# Every dog
# has its day

# Every dog has its day

## A thousand things you didn't know about man's best friend

### MAX CRYER

PUBLISHING

First published 2013

Exisle Publishing Limited,
P.O. Box 60-490, Titirangi, Auckland 0642, New Zealand.
'Moonrising', Narone Creek Road, Wollombi, NSW 2325, Australia.
www.exislepublishing.com

National Library of New Zealand Cataloguing-in-Publication Data
Cryer, Max.
Every dog has its day : A thousand things you didn't know
about man's best friend / Max Cryer.
Includes bibliographical references.
ISBN 978-1-921966-28-6
1. Dogs—Miscellanea. I. Title.
636.7—dc 23

ISBN 978-1-921966-28-6

10 9 8 7 6 5 4 3 2 1

Text design and production by IslandBridge
Cover design by Christabella Designs
Printed in China by Everbest Printing Co Ltd

---

All images www.shutterstock.com except for pages 31 and 47 (public domain through http://
en.wikipedia.org); page 84  < a href = "http://www.shutterstock.com/gallery-659047p1.
html?cr = 00&pl = edit-00" > Neftali < /a >  /  < a href = "http://www.shutterstock.
com/?cr = 00&pl = edit-00" > Shutterstock.com < /a; page 121 < a href = "http://
www.shutterstock.com/gallery-885118p1.html?cr = 00&pl = edit-00" > Nicku < /a >  /  < a
href = "http://www.shutterstock.com/?cr = 00&pl = edit-00" > Shutterstock.com < /a > ; pages 7
(bottom),13, 35 and 93 (IslandBridge); paw prints throughout (IslandBridge).

The author thanks

## Dame Kiri Te Kanawa

(whose suggestion initiated the project)

and

Geoffrey Pooch, Emma Sloman, Paul Barrett, Ian Watt,
Graeme & Valerie Fisher, Robbie Ancel, Clif Crane,
Pluto Stevens and Harry Stevens

## The Power of a Dog

When the fourteen years which Nature permits

Are closing in asthma, or tumour, or fits,

And the vet's unspoken prescription runs

To lethal chambers or loaded guns,

Then you will find – it's your own affair –

But ... you've given your heart to a dog to tear.

*Rudyard Kipling*

Man is a dog's idea
of what God should be.

*Holbrook Jackson*

Q Did you hear about
the dyslexic, agnostic,
insomniac?

A He lay awake at
night wondering if
there really was a Dog.

# Introduction

Throughout recorded history,
human beings have occupied a
position at the pinnacle of creation
and seen themselves as the main players
on the planet. But four other creatures have played
invaluable supporting roles in making this perception a
reality. Without the horse, the bullock, the dog and the cat, our
environment would be very different.

Before the industrial age, horses and bullocks contributed
muscle power in creating modern roads and railways. They
were also crucial in facilitating travel, supporting agriculture,
assisting in wars, and helping to build grand edifices before
cranes and front-end loaders were invented. Horses also
provided considerable profit (and loss) in their capacity as
racers, while the value of the relationships they formed with
humans cannot be underestimated.

Cats have never lifted a brick or hauled so much as a toy
cart, but they have provided companionship and solace to the
lonely, and are a haughty reminder to humans that they are
not always in charge. They never fail to intrigue the humans
they own.

But what of dogs? They have always been willing to provide, ungrudgingly, both work and companionship. Energetic and helpful, a dog can fulfil many roles. Or perhaps 'roles' is the wrong word, because a dog is not acting. It is for real, and is capable of being a fearsome guard, a diligent protector, a fashion accessory, a tireless herder of recalcitrant sheep or wandering cattle, a detective of secretive scents, a burglar alarm, a retriever of hunted quarry, a competitive racer, a guide for the blind and the deaf, a vital alert for those with allergies, an assistant to the law, a powerful hauler of snow vehicles, and a mobile smoke alarm. Songs are sung about them and, real or cartooned, they star in movies.

In addition to their rare capacity and willingness to work, they offer, seemingly without effort, impressive amounts of companionship and charm – not to mention bravery, humour, faithfulness and sometimes endearing eccentricity.

To many devoted dog owners, they are a form of god – the god spelt backwards.

# Citizen Canine

## The legend

When God created the universe, all the plants and animals came into being – but had no names. So during the seven days, the Almighty painstakingly gave a name to every creature that walked, swam, crawled and flew. Whether they had four legs, a tail, fins, wings, a tongue – He named them all.

The same applied to every plant that grew and climbed and spread and bloomed – the pine, the oak, the smallest bluebell – He named them all.

It was a tiring task, but eventually the Almighty had named every living creature on Earth.

Except one.

One animal had followed God throughout, faithfully keeping behind, always ready and never demanding. But no name had been given to him.

'Am I to be without a name?' he asked the Almighty.

God looked down, and said: 'I had not forgotten. You have been humble, you have been patient and you have waited your turn, like a good friend. So now I will give you a name – and to honour you, your name will be my own name – in reverse.

'You shall be called – Dog.'

## The fact

He may be man's best friend, but it is far from clear where his name comes from. The word 'dog' is one of the great mysteries in the English language.

It first appeared in print *c.1050* in the term *canum docgena*, but the origin of the word before that is obscure. Several European languages have words similar to *dog*, but these seem to be related to the English word and so provide no clue as to its original provenance.

Before the appearance of *dog*, the Old English word most commonly used to refer to canines was *hund*, or as we say today, *hound*. That can be found as early as *c.857* and was originally used to refer to any canines. Several centuries later, *hound* began to be used in the restricted sense we know today: a hunting dog, specialising in the chase, especially one that follows its prey by scent.

The female counterpart is *bitch*, a term which dates to *c.1000* and is believed to be related to an old Norse word *bikkja*. Using *bitch* as a derogatory term for a woman dates to some time before 1400. But despite its obscure origin, the word *dog*, like the canine it represents, has become an integral part of our lives.

# To say 'dog' in another language

| | |
|---|---|
| Arabic | **calb** |
| Bengali | **kukur** |
| Chinese | **gau** |
| Finnish | **koira** |
| Greek | **skylos** |
| Hebrew | **kelev** |
| Japanese | **seta** |
| Korean | **gae** |
| Latvian | **suns** |
| Polish | **pies** |
| Russian | **cobaka** |
| Serbian | **pas** |
| Tibetan | **khyi** |
| Zulu | **inja** |

And dogs don't always say *Bow-wow*, as the English language would have it – or *Yip-yip, Ruff-ruff* or *Arf*.

In Mandarin-speaking countries, dogs say *Wang-wang*, Romanian dogs say *Ham-ham,* and dogs in Russia say *Gav-gav*.

And there's more. Afrikaans: *Blaf-blaf;* Arabic: *Hau-hau*; Indonesian: *Guk-Guk*; Burmese: *Woke-woke*; Czech: *Haf-haf.* Israel's Hebrew-speaking dogs say *Hav-hav*, while dogs in Iceland say *Voff-vof*. In Korea they say *Meong-meon*. Spanish dogs say *Gua-gua* and Balinese people hear *Kong-kong*.

## Mongrel

Based on an ancient word meaning 'mixture', the word 'mongrel' has been through several mutations. In early years it was commonly seen as mungrell, but when Shakespeare's King Lear was printed in its First Quarto (1608), the bard wrote: 'a knave, beggar, coward, pandar, rascal, son and heir of a mongrill bitch.'

Spelling aside, it seems to indicate that that Shakespeare was the origin of the derogatory term 'son of a bitch'!

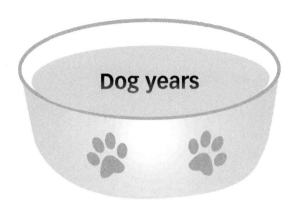

# Dog years

Calculating 'dog years' in relation to human years doesn't really work. Nobody seems to know how the notion arose that one year in a dog's life is the equivalent of seven years for a human. The comparison breaks down when you examine the facts.

First, a dog is likely to be sexually mature within one year, but a seven-year-old child is not. It could be another seven years before a child reaches a similar level of physical maturity. On that basis, a one-year-old dog could be seen as equivalent to a 14-year-old human. So right from the start the 7:1 ratio doesn't work. And since dogs vary enormously in size and breeds, with varying life expectancy, there cannot be a one-size-fits-all system to match them up with humans. Large and small dogs have different life expectancies. The short answer appears to be that there is no easy dog-to-human age conversion formula which close analysis can support.

# Hot dog

During the 1800s German
butchers introduced
Americans to a snack
produced by splitting a bun and
placing a hot sausage and some
sauce between the two halves. The
snack came to be known as a 'hot dog', but
the origins of the term are not entirely salubrious.

American word researcher David Popik discovered that
students at Yale became humorously suspicious about exactly
what kind of meat was being purveyed from the local snack
bars, which they began to call 'dog wagons'. The term 'hot
dog' appeared in the *Knoxville Daily Journal* (Tennessee) on
28 September 1883 and leapt to greater usage a year or so
later at Yale University. On 19 October 1895, the *Yale Record*
recorded an occasion where people 'contentedly munched hot
dogs during the whole service.' An iconic American name took
root.

A **corn dog** is a sausage coated in a thick layer
of cornmeal batter, then deep fried in oil (or
sometimes baked – a catalogue of American
cooking equipment in 1929 listed a *Krusty Korn
Dog Baker*). The sausage component is similar
to the other snack sausage known as a 'hot
dog' – but in a 'corn' version. When cooked in
its yellowish coating, the snack could be said
to resemble a ripe cob of corn.

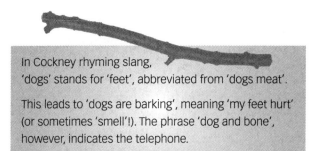

In Cockney rhyming slang, 'dogs' stands for 'feet', abbreviated from 'dogs meat'.

This leads to 'dogs are barking', meaning 'my feet hurt' (or sometimes 'smell'!). The phrase 'dog and bone', however, indicates the telephone.

## Hush puppies

In 1958 a sales manager for the Wolverine Shoe and Tanning Corporation was on a selling trip through the American states. When he reached the South, he was invited to a regional salesman's home for dinner. 'Hush-puppy' cornballs were part of the meal, and the sales manager asked, 'Why the name?' He was told about the practice of throwing the cornballs out the door 'to quiet the barking dogs'. The salesman was familiar with the informal way in which 'barking dogs' could sometimes refer to feet. At that time, the Wolverine company was in the process of launching a new type of casual shoe to be named 'Lasers'. But the sales manager immediately saw connections between aching feet – comfortable shoes – and cornballs keeping dogs quiet. The name 'Lasers' was dropped, and 'Hush Puppies' became an iconic name for the Wolverine company's new casual shoes.

Real 'hush puppies' are a cornmeal mix (sometimes with eggs, salt and milk) baked or deep-fried in oblong or spherical shapes, and popular in the Southern states of America as a side dish, often served with fish. They are also frequently thrown to domestic dogs when barking too much – in order to 'hush' them.

In the Middle Ages, dogs used in war were fitted with lightweight armour, as were hunting dogs (to protect them from attacks by wild boars or bears). The 'armour' was sometimes made from plates, or consisted of many layers of strong fabric reinforced with numerous metal eyelets. An armoured dog can be seen in an engraving by Alart du Hameel (*c.*1500) featuring the Emperor Constantine and a vision of the true cross. A version of **'dog armour'** still exists as protection for bush hunting. Made from high impact-resistant multi-layers of 'ballistic' fibre bound with nylon, the dog armour is strong but light, and banded with 'highlighter' strips.

**Chiengora** is the contrived name for dog hair spun into a soft yarn, then knitted into accessories: beanies, scarves, cardigans, gloves or sweaters – soft, warm, water-resistant (and a reminder of a favourite dog friend).

There is of course the slightly worrying thought that people wearing socks knitted from cast-off dog hair could be a focus for passing dogs unable to resist cocking their leg on the sock-wearer's ankles …

**Schnauzer** is derived from the German word *Schnauze* which means 'muzzle' or 'nose'. The English slang word 'schnoz' for nose has the same origin.

Leeds Castle in Kent is home to a museum-quality exhibition of more than a hundred dog collars, some over 500 years old. Fancy collars of velvet, silver and decorated leather are displayed next to 'hunting' collars made from iron and often spike-studded. These antique versions were intended to protect the dog's throat, in case of attack by aggressive wolves or boars.

Along with Oscars, Emmys, Tonys and Grammys, there is also an award for movie performances by dogs. At the Cannes Film festival the director of the voted best feature film is awarded the festival's highest honour, the Palme d'Or. In 2001 the international film critics instigated a further award, the **Golden Collar**, for the best performance by a canine. The Golden Collar award is literally a dog collar, spectacularly made of gold with Swarovski crystals. Curiously, the assessment of 'best performance' includes not only those by a real dog but animations too! (As yet the same liberal criterion does not apply to human performances.) Winners of the best (real) dog performance have included Uggie in *The Artist* and Koko in the Australian film *Red Dog*.

**Odie** is the rather gormless comic-strip beagle somewhat at odds with **Garfield**, the self-possessed cat. Odie and Garfield first appeared in 1978 and went on to be seen in 2500 newspapers as the world's most widely syndicated cartoon strip, earning over $700 million a year in imitative merchandise. Both Garfield and Odie started out walking on four paws, but gradually evolved into walking upright on only two.

The expression **'Every dog has his day'** offers the hope that everyone gets a chance eventually. An underling may rise to power – even temporarily – and enjoy 'a time in the sun'. Some scholars date the term to 405 BC but it didn't seem to reach print (in Greek) until Plutarch's *Moralia* (AD *c*. 95). Just over 1400 years later it made its first English appearance in Taverner's *Proverbes* (1539) as 'A dogge hath a day', and approximately 60 years later Shakespeare wrote in *Hamlet*: 'The cat will mew and dog will have his day.'

**'It shouldn't happen to a dog'.** In a strange kind of way this is a compliment to canines, in that something unpleasant is afoot and no one, not even a dog, should have to undergo it. Shakespeare uses the concept in *King Lear* when the Duke of Kent chides Regan: 'Why, madam, if I were your father's dog, You should not treat me so.'

New York's William Secord Gallery is the only gallery in the United States specialising in art depicting dogs. Fine nineteenth-century paintings, various-sized statues and prestige collectibles are its focus, as well as arranging portrait commissions between dog-owners and contemporary artists. Founder and dog aficionado William Secord has published five books on the social history of dog art and on some notable collections in the genre.

In Texas, north of Waco, a mall of antique shops (The Antiquibles) includes one which bills itself as the world's largest dog collectibles museum. With over 7000 items on display, the collection includes every kind of canine imagery: dog salt-and-pepper shakers, dog inkwells, dog buttons, dog figurines, a gun stock with a carved dog head, toys, walking canes, dog marionettes, and many representations of dogs in popular culture and advertising. Proprietress Barbara Hayes admits that 'I don't even try to keep them all dusted.'

In Washington DC, a comfortable drive from the White House, there is a pet museum – specifically pets of the Presidents. One of its most unusual exhibits is a portrait of Lucky, President Reagan's pet Bouvier des Flandres (Belgian Cattle Dog). But the portrait isn't photographed or painted – it is crafted out of Lucky's own hair, saved by dog groomer Clare McLean.

**The Bayeux Tapestry** (which is really an embroidery) is first mentioned in 1476, but may have been embroidered as early as 1070. It is over 70 metres long, and depicts 'the conquest of England' as perceived during that early era. Close examination of the tapestry reveals 626 human figures, 190 horses and 24 identifiable dogs. A further 30 creatures depicted *might* be dogs – but they could be wolves or foxes!

**'Barking up the wrong tree'** is an expression indicating that it would be a waste of energy to pursue a course of action which will not have the desired result. It has been in American use since 1830 and is believed to have arisen from racoon hunting – which is usually in the dark. A dog which has chased a racoon up a tree and loudly announced the fact may be unaware that high above him the racoon has jumped to another tree.

**'Call the dogs off'** means to cease some action or enquiry. This image is also from hunting, and arises from the huntsman seeing that his dogs are pursuing the wrong track (either 'barking up the wrong tree', as above, or, if fox-hunting, following a false trail) and calls them away from it. As a metaphor it indicates that a campaign of bothering, criticising, aggressively investigating, threatening or attacking is to be stopped.

# Whippet

The love of racing, and betting on it, covers all levels of social class and wealth. For many people in the north of England – hard working and distant from luxury – whippet dogs became known as the 'poor man's racehorse'. In early times they were raced informally out in open fields or along roads, often chasing a 'lure' of a scrap of cloth ... hence the term 'rag races'.

Fittingly, the name of the breed known as whippet is associated with speed. Etymologist Eric Partridge advises that its ultimate origin is the Latin *via*, meaning a road or pathway, which in English gives us such words as *viaduct*, *vibrate*, *convey*, *waiver*, *wiper* – and *whip*. The last – besides its obvious meaning as an accessory for cattlemen and other riders – developed an associated meaning of 'moving nimbly and fast'. So the swift and lively racing dog became a whippet.

In 1948, Swiss mountaineer George de Mestral came home from a hike with his beloved pet dog and laboriously picked out dozens of burrs from the dog's coat. Intrigued as well as irritated, he put some under a microscope and examined their thousands of tiny hooks, which could cling so tenaciously to another surface. This led him to experimenting with tape – one strip made to be 'hooked' and the other one 'looped'. When he got it to work, he turned his attention to a name. He borrowed two syllables from French: 'vel' from *velour* (velvet) and 'cro' from *crochet* (little hook). Thus was born **velcro**. Within a decade of its invention, 55 million metres a year were being produced.

'When a man's best friend is his dog, that dog has a problem.'
*Edward Abbey*

'Outside of a dog, a book is probably man's best friend; inside of a dog, it's too dark to read.'
*Groucho Marx*

In an Oriental restaurant if you notice the word *chien* on the menu, don't panic. In the Vietnamese language it means 'fried', and it sometimes turns up in a Korean or Chinese version with the same meaning.

**'Sundogs'** are an atmospheric phenomenon: bright spots that form about 22 degrees on either side of the sun from light reflecting off ice crystals in the clouds. The scientific name is *parhelion*, known colloquially as 'mock suns' or 'phantom suns'. They are best seen in icy areas when the sun is low on the horizon.

**It's raining cats and dogs.** There are several very doubtful explanations for this expression, including a belief that the bodies of dead cats and dogs floated in gutters during heavy rain; or that thatched roofs were a favourite resting place for household pets, which often fell through! Rather more probable is that the image is of Scandinavian origin and drifted into English from there. In ancient Northern European mythology, the god of war Odin was surrounded by wolves and dogs – and the dogs controlled the wind. Alongside this was the belief that witches' cats could transform themselves into natural forces. So when Odin's dogs became aggressive, and in the guise of wind chased the cats, the cats turned themselves into rain to escape the dogs. Most world cultures have inherited aspects of myth and legend (our Wednesday is named after Odin, for example) so the Scandinavian explanation is more likely to be correct than other more far-fetched suggestions.

**'Gone to the pack'** indicates that something or someone has deteriorated in some way; that a key feature about them is now less than it was. A perfectly healthy man might say his rugby playing has gone to the pack because he hasn't played for years; a fine pianist might say her keyboard technique has gone to the pack because she has three children under six and there just hasn't been time; or you might be told that a shop or business or newspaper has gone to the pack, meaning the whole thing is no longer as effective as it once was.

The expression draws on the fact that historically dogs are 'pack' animals, organised into levels of command, with distinct 'leaders' and 'followers'. If something has 'gone to the pack' the image is of a leader dog once full of virility and courage, but now failing and unable to keep up its prime position. The 'leader' has faded back among the 'followers' – the pack.

**'Gone to the dogs'** is similar in effect, indicating that a person has gone downhill socially in the worst way, like a street dog. The expression has two influencing factors. One is the practice of removing leftovers and food scraps from the table, or discarding provisions past their use-by date, and throwing them to the dogs. The result is a downgrading. But there is a second factor, from betting on dog-races. Betting can become an obsession and in some circumstances brings unrest and even financial difficulty. So 'going to the dogs' has yet another image of someone going downhill.

Charles Dickens in *Nicholas Nickleby* uses it in a faintly comic sense: someone has 'gone to the bow-wows'.

**'Old Shep'** is a 1933 song about a country boy and his faithful pet. As the boy ages into a man, Shep ages too – but becomes infirm. His death is marked by the classic lines:

If dogs have a heaven, there's one thing I know –
That Shep has a wonderful home.

The song later became a country music favourite. One of its early and notable performances was by a ten-year-old in a Mississippi-Alabama talent quest. In cowboy costume and standing on a chair, the lad's performance won him fifth place, $5 and free rides in a fairground. His name was Elvis Presley.

Willie Mae 'Big Mama' Thornton was a large blues singer with a dominating presence, thunderstorm voice and formidable charisma. In 1952 Mike Stoller and Jerry Lieber wrote a short song on the back of a paper bag, about a woman giving a very definite dismissal to a lover. They named it *'You ain't nothin' but a hound dog'*. Mama Thornton sang it with energetic passion, barking, howling and bellowing instructions to the band to wag their tails. In 1956 Elvis Presley heard her recording and added the song to his act. His first performance of the song on television was seen by 40 million people and caused an uproar, with critics using such terms as 'caterwaul' and 'no talent'. His next television performance was seen by an even bigger audience and he sang the song to a basset hound wearing a top hat.

**Dog in a manger** is a term arising from Aesop's *Fables*. Some hay has been put in a feeding trough or manger so the oxen can feed. But a bad-tempered dog decides to rest on the hay – and although he cannot eat hay himself, he snaps and snarls when the oxen try to reach their feed. The dog in the manger is preventing someone from having something they need or want, even though it is no use to him.

In his fourth inaugural address, President Franklin Roosevelt said:

'We have learned that we cannot live alone, at peace; that our own well being is dependent on the well being of other nations far away. We have learned that we must live as men, not as ostriches, nor as dogs in the manger.'

**Salukis** were named after the ancient city of Saluq in Libya. The breed is also known as the Persian Greyhound and the Royal Dog of Egypt.

**Dog tags** are metal identity tags worn by military personnel. Historically, servicemen customarily carried some form of personal identity, either on paper or sewn into their clothing. In 1870 the Prussian army introduced tags nicknamed *Hundemarken* (dog licence disc) based on Berlin's system of licensing canines. By 1898 American soldiers were buying their own version, manufactured privately. In 1906 the US Army introduced formal aluminium 'dog tags' to be worn under clothing at all times.

**Helping a lame dog over a stile** is showing a rather more generous disposition than that of the dog in the manger. It means to show a kindness and help someone in distress. But it is often heard in the negative, describing someone *un*kind who is deemed selfishly *un*likely to help a lame dog (or a lame anybody else) over a stile.

**'Cry havoc, and let slip the dogs of war.'**
Shakespeare's famous line is from *Julius Caesar*, *c.*1601. 'Havoc' was a military call in early times, a signal for plundering and fighting to begin, while 'dogs of war' is believed to have been Shakespeare's metaphor for the fighting men, the soldiery.

# The Canary Islands

The Canary Islands off the west coast of Africa have had other names throughout history: Happy Islands, Garden of the Hesperides, Atlantida. There is even a belief that this might have been the fabled Atlantis. In ancient times when the Romans came to the islands they encountered fierce natives – and their dogs. The Latin for dog is *canis*, and when referring to the place the Romans used the word *Canaria* because of the dogs. The name stuck – and the islands' official symbol now shows two dogs holding a shield containing symbols of seven of the main islands, surmounted by a crown (the Canaries are part of the kingdom of Spain).

Although the Canary Islands are named after dogs, there is in fact a strong connection with the canary bird. The little birds are native to islands in the Atlantic – including the Azores, Madeira and the Canary Islands. When the wild birds were introduced into England as charming household singing pets from the Canary Islands, they were referred to by the name of the islands, so the name of the bird, like the islands, is derived from the Latin word for dog!

In spite of its name, **Dogger Bank** has no connection with dogs. It is a large sandbank in a shallow area of the North Sea off the east coast of England. *Encyclopedia Britannica* states that the name derives from the old two-masted trawling vessel known to the Dutch as a *dogger*.

**The Isle of Dogs** is a district in London – on a peninsula intruding into the River Thames. Formerly an island, it is now accessible by causeway and/or tunnel. The name has been known since the late 1500s – and possibly earlier – though any association with dogs is unclear. Legend has it that King Edward III kept his hounds there in *c.*1140, as Henry VIII possibly did in *c.*1530.

Another theory is that in an earlier century an influx of engineers from Holland helped reclaim land in London, giving rise to the name the Isle of Dutch, which was later corrupted. Yet another belief is that this area of the Thames was a favourite haunt of waterfowl, hence the Isle of Ducks, also later corrupted. Nobody knows for sure.

**Sick as a dog** is but one of a series of 'sick as ...' expressions which variously refer to a horse, a cat, a rat and a parrot. 'Sick as a dog' is the oldest known of these, dating from 1592, and can be taken at face value to mean an unwell dog, but there may also be an underlying wish to give 'a bad press' to dogs. There is of course some basis for this, because in 1592 'sick' was often a synonym for 'vomit' – something dogs are known to do as a result of their adventurous and less than selective eating habits. And when they feel the need to void, they simply do it wherever they may be. (Some also return to what they voided, a phenomenon twice mentioned in the Bible: Proverbs 26:11; 2 Peter 2:22.)

**Hair of the dog that bit you** is an expression meaning that a small repeat dose of whatever caused a malady will effect its cure. It is based on an ancient belief that rust obtained from a spear which caused injury will help heal that same injury if mixed with ointment and applied to it. From this arose the notion that if a dog bit you, some hairs from that same dog, if placed on the wound, would help it heal. A further deviation is the firm conviction that a small whisky on the morning of a severe hangover will waft it away ...

# His Master's Voice

 How did a deceased English pet become so recognisable worldwide? When English painter Francis Barraud played his phonograph, his dog Nipper (who was inclined to nip ankles) always looked puzzled about the source of the noise. Nipper died in 1895, but lived on fondly in Barraud's memory, so much so that four years later Barraud painted a picture of Nipper paying attention to a cylinder phonograph. It occurred to him that the picture might be useful for advertising, so he approached the Edison-Bell company. They declined, saying that 'dogs don't listen to phonographs'.

But while investigating a new phonograph horn from the alternative Gramophone Company he mentioned the picture again, and was told that if he would change the cylinder phonograph in the picture to the more modern *disc* gramophone, they would be interested. He did, and they were. The company bought the picture and copyrighted it in 1900 as 'His Master's Voice'. The image would become one of the most famous advertising symbols in the world.

An American electrician called James Spratt arrived in England in 1860 and noticed dogs on the wharf munching scraps of hard sea biscuits. He saw a sales opportunity, and devised a baked mixture of meat, vegetables and flour. 'Spratt's Dog Cakes' were an enormous success – and became the ancestor of dog biscuits.

One Spratt's salesman in England sold biscuits to the kennels at stately homes and country manors. Mainly because the biscuits appealed to the owners of pure-bred dogs, he became interested in dog 'quality'. His name was Charles Cruft. He left his sales job and in 1891 established a show. Crufts now attracts entries from all over the world – at last count numbering well over 20,000 dogs.

The word **pedigree**, meaning a genealogical table or the line of descent of a purebred animal, is derived from an old French expression *pied de grue* – the foot of a crane bird. A resemblance was perceived between a crane's foot and the spreading lines of a family chart.

# The Crufts Dog Show

The Crufts dog show in Britain features only pedigree purebreds, and generates enormous interest from dog owners and breeders. But in 2000, the Kennel Club recognised that dogs can also be fun and a source of pride and companionship, regardless of how random their family tree might be. So a second show evolved, entitled Scruffts.

Aristocratic lineage is not required. Indeed, judges are forbidden to mention connection to (or absence from) any recognisable breed. Instead, classes for entry include Child's Best Friend; Golden Oldie Crossbreed; Most Handsome Crossbreed; Waggingest Tail and Prettiest Bitch. The entry fee for each class is modest, and proceeds go to the Kennel Club Charitable Trust. Scruffts prelims are held at fifteen venues in the UK, and class winners make a guest appearance at the huge annual Discover Dogs show. One hundred and ninety pedigree dogs take part – and the cheerfully non-pedigree (but much loved) Scruffts winners make guest appearances.

A **dogleg** is a sharp bend in a road, graph or design. The amplified version is 'like a dog's hind leg'.

A **dog ear**, apart from belonging to an actual dog, commonly refers to the folded-down corner of a page in a book – as if like a dog's ear flopping over. However, the expression is not entirely accurate, because many breeds of dogs have ears which stand up.

Names for the various shapes of ear which different breeds have:

| | |
|---|---|
| pricked | standing upright |
| button | semi-upright, with the top portion folded downwards |
| bat | fully standing, wide and facing forward |
| candle flame | upright, very wide at the base and narrowing upwards to a distinct tip |
| drop | falling down in a fold from where they join the head |
| pendant | the whole ear hangs loosely down the side of the face |
| rose | small drop ears which fold over pointing backwards |
| tulip | upright with the edges curved inwards |
| blunt-tips | the top part of the ear rounded rather than pointed. |

**A dog's tongue** has quite a responsibility. It conveys food and water, responds to taste, touch and pain, helps heal wounds, communicates diverse messages, and replaces sweating with panting as a temperature regulator. There are eight pairs of muscles to activate it and five pairs of nerves which come straight from the brain. Four pairs of salivary glands help keep the tongue wet, aided by many smaller saliva-producing sources on the tongue surface.

The method by which dogs drink is not exactly tidy. Dogs stick their tongue into the fluid then curl the tongue downwards and inwards, making a little 'pouch' *underneath* the tongue – which is then quickly brought back into the mouth with a gulp. Imbibing the water on the underside  of the tongue in this rather precarious way often results in excess water being splashed about. So besides being noisy, drinking dogs can be messy. However, if the liquid is thicker, say of gravy or porridge-like consistency, the dog changes tack and moves the tongue below the solution, lifting it on to the tongue's upper surface.

## Ears

On the complex subject of a dog's hearing, it is safe to say the dog can hear with approximately ten times more efficiency than a human. By one estimate, dogs can locate the source of a sound in 0.06 of a second. Their ears have many sensory nerves – which is a good reason not to blow playfully into them. Gentle though the blowing may be, and even though *you* can scarcely hear it, the level of amplification inside the ear is enough to cause distress to the dog.

A dog has whiskers on its muzzle, under its jaw and over its eyes. Known as *vibrissae*, they are sensitive to changes in 'air dynamics'.

## Teeth

Dogs normally have 42 teeth (humans have 32, female horses 40, male horses 42). The average dog has a biting pressure of 150 lbs (68 kgs) or more. A really big dog can summon up 450 lbs pressure (240 kgs) per square inch.

**Flews** are the large upper lips which, on certain dogs (e.g. the greyhound), hang down pendulously.

**A dew-claw**, sometimes called a 'dog thumb', is the little claw behind a dog's foot.

## Eyes

Depending on the breed, a dog's field of vision can range from 120 degrees to 270 – somewhat wider than a human's. However, the upper range is found only in some breeds, notably the greyhound. The norm is between 120 to 180 degrees. But of that 'seeing area' only a proportion is in 'binocular' vision – where the perception area of one eye overlaps that of the other eye, giving a clear-focused three-dimensional view.

At the back of a dog's retina is a structure called the *tapetum lucidum* – which is a kind of biological mirror reflecting whatever light is available back through the retina, thus having the effect of increasing even a small amount of light. This enhances the dog's night vision.

Along with birds, amphibians, reptiles and some other mammals (but not humans), dogs have a third eyelid: the nictitating membrane (or 'haw'). When foreign matter comes into the eye, the haw moves across the eye sideways as a kind of windscreen wiper.

**'The more I see of men, the more I love dogs.'**

This worthy philosophy has been attributed to many different people, depending on which book of quotations you pick up. Its origins appear to be French. In the late 1600s the Marquise de Rabutin-Chantal, better known as Madame de Sévigné, wrote in a letter to her daughter: *Plus je connais les hommes, plus j'aime les chiens* – 'The more I know of men, the more I love dogs.'

Decades later, in 1740, King Frederick the Great of Prussia offered a version: 'The more I see of men, the better I like my dog.' (Frederick owned an estimated 30 greyhounds and certainly loved them – he instructed that he was to be buried next to his beloved greyhounds.) In 1765 Pierre Belloy and Voltaire both took up the notion that the company of dogs was often preferable to that of people.

From then on a who's who are credited with originating the phrase: French political activist Madame Jeanne-Marie Roland, Baroness Madame de Stael, and French writer Alphonse de Lamartine. Some even attribute the sentiment to General Charles de Gaulle! The quote from him (in English) slightly amplifies the original: 'The better I get to know men, the more I find myself loving dogs.'

The list doesn't end there. Different sources credit the line to Joussenel, Erik Satie, Sacha Guitry and American lawyer Gloria Allred. Doubtless all of them support the sentiment, but it would appear that all of them are actually quoting Madame de Sévigné.

# Dog faeces

Dog faeces contain an element which assists in the softening of skins during the production of leather. In the nineteenth century there was a ready market for the sale of dog faeces in cities with a tannery. Henry Mayhew, in *London Labour and the London Poor* (1851), writes that the people collecting the faeces were graced with the name 'pure-finders' — 'pure' because their goods purified leather (rather than the gatherers themselves). The pure-finders carried a basket, generally with a cover to hide the contents, and their right hand was covered with a black leather glove. However, Mayhew reports that 'many of them dispense with the glove, as they say it is much easier to wash their hands than to keep the glove fit for use.'

The pure-finders sold their collections by the bucketful to tanneries, where the 'dry limey sort' fetched the highest price because of its higher alkaline quality. A city with tanneries might have as many as 200 pure-finders busy collecting dog poo – ultimately to enable books to be beautifully bound, purses and pocket-books to be flexible, and ladies to wear fine kid gloves and delicate lightweight shoes.

The practice was widespread and much older than nineteenth-century Britain. *An Entertaining Tale of Quadrupeds*, a poem written in the fourteenth century, traces it back as far as Byzantine times. But by the end of the nineteenth century, leather technician Joseph Turney Wood had discovered more sanitary chemical ways of curing leather, and gradually the pure-finders were no more.

**Papillon** is a particular breed of spaniel. It takes its name from the French word for 'butterfly', because of the appearance of its high-sitting fringed ears. A papillon with dropped ears is called a phalène, which is French for 'moth'.

**Terrier** is derived from the old French *chien terrier* ('dog of the earth'), with *terrier* coming from the Latin *terra* – earth. It was so named for its diligence in pursuing quarry into or out of the earth.

The **Jack Russell terrier** and the **Parson Russell terrier** are both named after the Reverend John Russell, who bought and then bred from a small terrier early in the nineteenth century.

**Pinscher** comes from the German word for 'terrier', though sometimes it is seen as a reference to the German region of Pinzgau.

**Doberman**(n) is named after Friedrich Louis Dobermann, a German tax collector who realised he needed some protection from being robbed while doing his collecting. He bred Manchester terriers with pinschers, and rottweilers with greyhounds, until finally producing the doberman (the final 'n' of his name gradually faded away).

**Rottweilers** are named after the German town of Rottweil which, during an early Roman occupation of the area, had many villas with red-tiled roofs. Hence the name *Rott* (signifying red) and *weil* (roof). The dogs have a long history of herding livestock, pulling carts of butchered meat to market, and guarding the butcher's takings in leather pouches tied around their neck.

Louis de Loménie reports that **Pierre Beaumarchais**, author of *The Barber of Seville* (the original play – the opera came later), didn't believe in anything as simple as a collar having just a dog's name inscribed on it. The wording on his pet's collar read:

> 'I am Mademoiselle Follette; Beaumarchais belongs to me; We live on the boulevard.'

Belgian poet **Henri Michaux** (1899-1984) pointed out that you never see a dog smelling a rose or a violet. Instead, their interest lies in odours rather more foul:

> 'They carry a goddam dossier in their heads, constantly updated. Who understands the menu of stink better? They think about it … Got it! Now they know!'

French author **Charles Baudelaire** was of a similar mind. In *The Dog and the Flask* he wrote that when he summoned his dog to sniff from a flask of expensive perfume, the dog bounded up with its tail wagging in anticipation. But when the stopper was removed and the costly scent released, the dog lurched back in dismay, with barks of distress. In exasperation, Baudelaire mused that if instead the dog had been offered a pile of poo, he would have sniffed it with delight … and very likely eaten it!

Baudelaire also made a rather uncomplimentary comparison between his dog and the general public, which he declared must always be presented with 'carefully selected scraps of nastiness', instead of 'delicious perfumes which only exasperate it'.

**Throw it to the dogs**. In other words, something is useless, so get rid of it. Shakespeare's Macbeth tells his doctor: 'Throw physic to the dogs – I'll have none of it.'

The dog known as a **lurcher** is a swift and silent hound. Believed to have been bred by gypsies from an unorthodox mix of greyhound, collie and terrier, it is said to be favoured by poachers. The name comes from *lur*, the Romany gypsy word for 'thief'. According to *The Guinness Book of Records*, a lurcher once cleared a wire fence 8ft 9ins high (2.66 m) in one jump.

**'Houndstooth'** is the name given to a textile pattern originated in woven wool in the lowlands of Scotland. It consists of recurring figures of 'broken check' made up of abstract four-pointed shapes. Seen most strikingly in black and white, it is now found the world over in various colours and configurations, and in clothing ranging from haute couture to traditional chef pants (the design helps obscure smudges and stains). A smaller-scale version of the original traditional check, known as 'puppytooth', is also available.

**The Dickin Medal** was inaugurated in 1943 to honour animals which had served in war or civil defence. The medal features two inscriptions: *For Gallantry* and *We Also Serve*. Colloquially referred to as the 'animals' Victoria Cross', over the years it has been awarded for outstanding service to three horses, 27 dogs, 32 pigeons and one cat. In 2011 the medal was received by Treo, a Labrador which located improvised explosive devices (IEDs) while serving with the Royal Veterinary Corps in Afghanistan.

# The World Trade Centre

When terrorists attacked the World Trade Centre in New York on 11 September 2011, few could have predicted the role dogs would play in the rescue effort.

Apollo, a German Shepherd, was the first of the New York Police K9 Search and Rescue team to arrive at what is now called Ground Zero. He began work just 15 minutes after the initial attack. Tireless and obedient, he worked through extraordinarily difficult conditions, enduring fire and falling debris. At one point he stumbled into a pool, which actually saved him from a sudden outburst of flames, since he was soaking wet.

Over 300 dogs were brought to the site – in addition to two which were already there. Roselle and Salty were

two golden Labrador seeing-eye dogs, who were in the building with their blind owners, Omar Rivera and Michael Hingson, when the tragedy struck. Remaining calm after the attack, they saved their owners' lives by guiding them down 71 flights of stairs through virtually impenetrable smoke, reaching safety just before the entire building collapsed.

Only one dog lost his life in the search and rescue efforts. This was Sirius, attached to the Port Authority Police Department.

While the efforts of all 300 dogs were lauded in the devastating aftermath of the attack, Apollo, Roselle and Salty were awarded the Dickin Medal for outstanding bravery and devotion.

# Heroes

Disabled by a car accident in 1995, British man Gareth Jones became accustomed to and adept at using his wheelchair, in company with his 'service dog'. But the dog's training didn't include towing or hauling – until Mr Jones crossed a field which proved too muddy for his wheelchair. It sank, and he found himself firmly stuck in a location remote from any possible human help. So Gareth Jones found a cord tucked somewhere within his chair and threw one end to the golden retriever, not sure if the dog would figure out what was required. The dog figured it out immediately, took the rope-end between his teeth, pulled with all his might, and kept on pulling until Mr Jones and his chair were in the clear. The retriever, appropriately named Hero, was given an All-Star Animal Award in London for his devotion and enterprise.

In 2008 a man phoned the police from a rural area near La Plata, Argentina, and reported that he had heard a baby's cries coming from a nearby field. He had investigated, and to his astonishment found a dog with six puppies – and a human baby tucked up among them. Buenos Aires police later traced the baby's 14-year-old mother, who was in need of psychological treatment and had abandoned her baby. The dog came to the rescue and carried the child 50 metres away to join her own offspring. The night was very cold, and medical staff later said the baby was little damaged from the passage across the field in a dog's mouth, and would undoubtedly have died of the cold without the animal's temporary protection.

**Dog paddle** is a simple swimming style characterised by the swimmer lying chest-down and moving their hands and legs alternately in a downwards 'scoop' fashion, similar to the way dogs and other animals swim. The style is preferred by those who proficient swimmers describe as 'not wishing to get their faces wet'.

Koreans have a proverb: 'A nobleman though drowning would never dog paddle.'

In March 1977, workmen boarded up a supposedly empty house in Worcestershire, UK, unaware that a bitch named Beauty and her puppy were still inside. Unable to escape, the dogs were without food, water or warmth for several days. By this time Beauty was desperate, so she tried the only escape outlet she could see. From the open fireplace, she wedged herself into the chimney, and somehow struggled up 45 ft (20.4 m) to open air on the roof. Impassioned barking drew the attention of someone passing by, and the pair were released to their owners – who lived next door and had no idea where Beauty and her pup had got to.

### Oh where, oh where has my little dog gone?

In 1864 American musician Septimus Winner put new words to an old German song, which was originally about a young man who had lost a sock ('Zu Lauterbach hab' ich mein Strumpf verloren'). Winner's English version changed it to a more plaintive lament about a lost pet. Over time the line 'With his ears cut short and his tail cut long' proved a concern, so 'cut' is often discreetly replaced with 'so'.

## Once upon a time

The ancient city of Pompeii near Naples was buried under a thick layer of volcanic ash during an eruption in AD 79. Later excavation revealed precious knowledge about the everyday life of the ancient inhabitants of the Mediterranean region. For example, evidence was found that households gave warning about the presence of a dog. In one building, a mosaic of a large and fearsome-looking dog was accompanied by the Latin slogan *Cave Canem*, which tells us that 'Beware of the Dog' was an admonition used 2000 years ago.

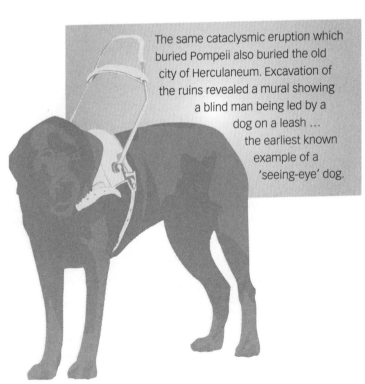

The same cataclysmic eruption which buried Pompeii also buried the old city of Herculaneum. Excavation of the ruins revealed a mural showing a blind man being led by a dog on a leash ... the earliest known example of a 'seeing-eye' dog.

# Hearing and
# therapy dogs

Guiding the blind is not the only way that a dog's judgement and sensory qualities can help humans. Assistance dogs for the deaf can be trained to attract their owner if a phone rings, a door knocker is heard, a baby cries or a smoke alarm sounds.

Furthermore, visits from friendly well-behaved dogs known as 'therapy dogs' have been found to bring a distinct uplift to residents of rest homes and patients in hospitals and hospices. People feeling isolated, restless or unhappy can respond with pleasure when a calm and amiable dog lays its head on a knee or a bedside. Nursing homes, care residences for the disabled (including the mentally disabled) welcome the almost immediate pleasure a dog's visit can bring to patients, and if the same dog's visits are regular the animal will often be regarded by the patient as their friend – sometimes their only friend. People enduring high-pressure business situations, intense times at university or post-military trauma acknowledge that sessions in the company of a dog can bring stress levels down. Many places in the world now have established 'therapy dog networks' which organise visiting programmes with appropriate institutions.

# Fashion

In 1986 Ilene Hochberg published a parody of the world's most famous fashion magazine. Called *Dogue*, its entire contents, including beauty advice, hairstyles, seasonal sportswear, letters to the editor, fashion news, events and advertising, featured only dog models and language meticulously adjusted to suit. Four-legged readers were advised how to 'put on the dog' with the latest styles from Canine Klein, Karl Dogerfield, Ruff Lauren, Christian Doig, Yves St Bernard and Oscar de la Rawhide. New lines of cosmetics from Rufflon promised to make the 'difference between a dog and a *hot* dog!' And for grand events, *haute canine* jewellery from Van Cleef & Arfpel … or Bulldogari.

> The upmarket New York shop Neiman Marcus offers bed pillows for dogs to sleep on. They come in 38 different combinations of fabric and design.

For the discerning dog traveller (or the owner), Louis Vuitton makes a high-fashion *Sac Chien*, a travel bag especially designed for the portable dog. It has a fold-back top for the pooch that likes to look around, and a side mesh panel with an optional roll-down cover when the pet prefers privacy. The bag comes in Vuitton's distinct patterning, and at a high-fashion price. Monograms of the owner's (or the dog's) initials may be added at an extra cost.

## Space travel

From 1949 onwards, many dogs took part in Russian suborbital rocket travel, with experimental flights continuing for six more years. Scientists chose female dogs to take part in the experiments because in the confined interior space they did not need to lift a leg to urinate. In 1957 the huskie-mix Laika became the first living creature to be launched into earth orbit and make a complete space orbit around the world, at a height of 1050 miles (1690 kms). Her presence in the craft provided valuable information to the ground-based Russian scientists in planning further experiments for sending a human into space. There was no recovery method for orbital space flights at the time and the scientists knew that Laika could not be brought back to earth. She was the only dog Russians sent into space knowing that she must die. It is believed that a discreet arrangement was made for her oxygen to run out at a prescribed point during the five-month orbit, in the hope that her death would be without stress.

**President John F. Kennedy** was given a dog by Russian premier Nikita Khrushchev. She was Pushinka, whose mother Strelka had been in space. Pushinka mated with a White House terrier, giving rise to what the President called a litter of 'pupniks'.

**A doggy bag** is a container into which the remains of a restaurant meal are put for 'taking home to the dog' … or maybe the diner fancies a snack later.

British beef farmer Marjorie Walsh, author of *Cooking For Dogs*, sells high-end Scottish/Kobe fillet, rib roast and sirloin steak, then transforms the lesser cuts into 'special occasion' foods for dogs, such as birthday cakes made with brisket and topside. Flavours can be molasses, eastern spices, carob or aniseed (which she identifies as 'the catnip of the dog world'). And they're personalised: if a photo of the birthday dog is provided, it is printed in edible ink on the icing. For dessert there is fish-flavoured ice cream and peanut-butter biscuits. Very considerately, all the ingredients are selected so that humans can share the birthday treats with their dogs.

# Doggy treats

Australians who like their dogs to live well can certainly find treats at the Diamond Dog Bakery in Melbourne, which specialises in creating imaginative *haute cuisine* for pooches. Their specialities include: breakfast foods for dogs, dogs' barbecue meals, biscuits of bacon and cheese, chicken meatballs, pupperoni pizza, doggie doughnuts, and dinners of turkey and cranberry or tuna and kelp. Fido's birthday guests can munch on pupcorn, and once a year there are Christmas plum puddings for pooches (minus raisins and sultanas, which can be harmful to dogs). Also available are recipes for lentil loaf and chickpea balls … for those owners who prefer their dogs to be vegan.

The lifestyle gap between rural dogs and their urban cousins is never more apparent than on a visit to a city pet shop. Apart from extensive shelves of 'dog toys', there are also dog toothbrushes (attached to the top of a firm plastic finger-stall, for the owner to administer) accompanied by beef-flavoured toothpaste. There is shampoo and conditioner in fragrances of chamomile and strawberry. A plastic 'peeing post' treated with a pheromone persuades the dog to pee wherever you put the post – rather than wherever the dog might want to.

Some pet shops in America offer even more attentive dog care: pasta packs with lamb, duck or turkey sauce, doggy ice cream, and apple-pie flavoured biscuits shaped like cats and postmen. Pets' health is also to the fore. For dogs who need 'weight management' there are low-calorie foods and aromatherapy sprays to help 'retain and improve their emotional balance'. Appointments can also be made for dogs to have acupuncture.

# Books

One of P.G. Wodehouse's recurring characters is Bartholomew, an Aberdeen terrier. Bartholomew does not strike affection in the heart of Bertie Wooster, who views the terrier somewhat unkindly as 'a canine excrescence' with a 'superior sanctimonious expression on his face' – a face which is 'fitted out with the jaws and teeth of a crocodile'. In *Stiff Upper Lip, Jeeves*, Bertie recounts that:

> 'Aberdeen terriers, possibly owing to their heavy eyebrows, always seem to look at you as if they were in the pulpit of the church of a particularly strict Scottish sect, and you were a parishioner of dubious reputation sitting in the front row of the stalls.'

Unlike Bertie Wooster, President Franklin Roosevelt so loved his Aberdeen terrier (known also as a Scottish terrier) that the affectionate little dog went everywhere with him – and appears sitting by him in the bronze statue commemorating Roosevelt's presidency.

In P.G. Wodehouse's story *Mike and Psmith visit Clapham*, Mike is talked into accompanying Psmith to a Socialist rally on Clapham Common. On arrival, he is nervous that the atmosphere is slightly hostile. Wodehouse captures the moment by describing that Mike 'proceeded to the meeting with the air of an about-to-be-washed dog'.

American humorist Franklin P. Jones once advised: 'Anybody who doesn't know what soap tastes like never washed a dog.'

**Timmy** the dog is the fifth member of the Famous Five in Enid Blyton's famous series of books. A loyal and faithful mongrel, Timmy made his debut in 1942 and then appeared in 20 other books in the series. They have sold over 100 million copies.

Mark Haddon's book *The Curious Incident of the Dog in the Night-time* won him the 2003 Whitbread Book of the Year and the 2004 Commonwealth Writers' Prize. The book is a first-person narrative by a 15-year-old boy who tells us he has 'behaviour difficulties'. Within his story the words 'autism', 'savant' and 'Asperger's syndrome' are never mentioned, but the book attracted wide attention because of its careful portrayal of a person within that framework.

*The Curious Incident of the Dog in the Night-time* takes its title from a line in the Sherlock Holmes story *Silver Blaze* (1894). In the story, Holmes asserts that whoever stole the famous racing horse Silver Blaze during the night was familiar in the stable area, because the dog had not barked during the night. Thus the thief must be someone the dog knew well.

The Scottish/Aberdeen terrier is the model for the 'dog' piece in the game of Monopoly.

**Milou ('Snowy')** is the faithful fox terrier who accompanies Tintin, the fictional Belgian cartoon character created by Georges Remi. The Tintin cartoons have been translated into 50 languages and the Tintin books have sold over two hundred million copies.

When Charlotte Brontë's character **Jane Eyre** returns to Thornfield Hall after many years, she finds her former employer Mr Rochester, whom she had never stopped loving, is blind. He is always accompanied by his old dog, Pilot. Unannounced, Jane Eyre takes Mr Rochester's supper tray into the room. Instantly:

> Pilot pricked up his ears when I came in: then he jumped up with a yelp and a whine, and bounded towards me: he almost knocked the tray from my hands. I set it on the table; then patted him, and said softly, 'Lie down!' Mr Rochester turned mechanically to see what the commotion was: but as he saw nothing, he returned and sighed.

Thus began one of the most famous reunions in English literature, with love requited.

**Sir Walter Scott's** favourite dog was the very large Maida – a metre tall and nearly two metres long from nose-tip to tail-base. According to *The New York Times* (1898), Maida was a cross between a wolfhound and a greyhound. He was named after the Battle of Maida fought between British troops and the French Empire during the Napoleonic wars. Scott talked to him as he was writing – as if seeking opinion on his current work. When Maida died in 1824, Sir Walter had a marble figure of the dog laid atop the grave, with the inscription:

> *Maidae. Marmorea dormis sub imagine*
> *Maida, Ad ianuam domini sit tibi terra levis.*

Beneath the sculpted form which late you wore,
Sleep soundly Maida, at your master's door.

**Dandie Dinmont** is the only dog breed named after a fictional character. In Sir Walter Scott's novel *Guy Mannering* (1814), Dandie Dinmont is a farmer with terriers, to whom he gives names like 'Old Pepper' and 'Little Mustard'. Dinmont asserts that his terriers can cope with stoats and weasels as well as 'rottens, tods, and brocks' (rats, foxes and badgers): 'They fear naething that ever cam' wi' a hairy skin on 't.' The book was so successful that the breed was named after the character.

The song **'Mad Dogs and Englishmen'** was introduced to the world in New York in 1931, sung by Beatrice Lillie on Broadway. Since then it has always been associated with its composer, Noël Coward. But its origins date back much further than 1931. *The Oxford Magazine* of 1772 (vol. 4) carries the line:

> It is a common thing to hear a Spaniard say, in most of the cities of Spain, that 'none but English men and dogs are seen in their streets immediately after dinner'.

Over 120 years later and half a world away, in 1901, Rudyard Kipling observed in his novel *Kim*:

> Only the devil and the English walk to and fro without reason.
> *and*
> We walk as though we were mad – or English.

Thirty years later Sir Noël Coward took up the image from the previous two observers. All credit to him for transforming it into an iconic song with impressive command of both external and internal rhyme.

Within the somewhat unlikely context of his song *Stinkfoot*, **Frank Zappa** introduces the character of a dog who can talk – and not just idle talk, but rather surreal and philosophical discourse. Zappa quotes Fido as saying:

> Once upon a time
> Somebody say to me
> What is your Conceptual Continuity?
> Well, I told him right then
> It should be easy to see
> The crux of the biscuit
> Is the Apostrophe …

In the commentary included with their CD *Celebrate*, the American rock group **Three Dog Night** explains the group's name. Vocalist Danny Hutton's girlfriend of the time had been reading about Australian Aborigines. She told the rockers that on cold nights the Aborigines would customarily keep a dog close to them for warmth. On colder nights they would sleep with two dogs, and if the night was freezing it would be a 'three dog night'.

If the young woman had read something else (say, William J. Burroughs' *Climate Change in Prehistory*) she might have discovered that the term was also commonly used by the Chukchi people (who originated the husky breed) in eastern Siberia, which is certainly a great deal colder than anywhere in Australia. Other races have also reportedly used dog duvets, but the connection with an American rock group made Australia the front runner.

**Dog days.** The ancient Romans linked the rising of the star Sirius in July and August with their nation's sultry summer heat. They believed that the star's bright visibility at that time of year added to the heat of the sun. Sirius is part of the constellation known as *Canis Major* (The Great Dog), so Sirius became known as the 'dog star'. By extension, the peak of summer came to be known as 'the dog days'. The relationship does not hold any validity in the southern hemisphere, where summer is from December to February.

## Cerberus, guard dog of Hades

In ancient Greek mythology, Cerberus is the watchdog chained to the gates of Hades or Hell. He harasses the spirits entering Hades and devours those who try to escape. In spite of the lack of first-hand reports, it is widely believed that Cerberus had three heads. The centre head was the shape of a lion's, while the other two resembled those of a dog and a wolf. Keeping the heads warm is a mane of writhing live snakes, while his tail is no ordinary dog's tail – it has the lethal whip of a dragon. It was the twelfth labour of Hercules to go to the depths of Hades and kill Cerberus.

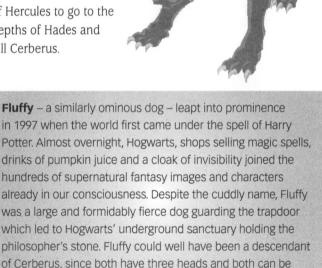

**Fluffy** – a similarly ominous dog – leapt into prominence in 1997 when the world first came under the spell of Harry Potter. Almost overnight, Hogwarts, shops selling magic spells, drinks of pumpkin juice and a cloak of invisibility joined the hundreds of supernatural fantasy images and characters already in our consciousness. Despite the cuddly name, Fluffy was a large and formidably fierce dog guarding the trapdoor which led to Hogwarts' underground sanctuary holding the philosopher's stone. Fluffy could well have been a descendant of Cerberus, since both have three heads and both can be lulled to sleep by music (Fluffy quite likes harp music).

**Argos** (sometimes Argus) was the faithful dog owned by Odysseus, King of Ithaca, in Homer's *Odyssey*. When Odysseus returns from his twenty years of voyages and fighting in the Trojan wars, his house has been overtaken and the servants have ceased to care. Odysseus disguises himself as a beggar to enter the premises unobserved. As he approaches his house, an old, abandoned, flea-infested dog, lying weak and dying on a dung heap, pricks up his ears. It is Argos – once Odysseus's faithful and swift hunting dog. Undeterred by the long absence and the disguise, Argos recognises Odysseus at once and has just enough strength to wag his tail – but is too weak to get up to greet his master. Having seen his master once more after twenty years, Argos 'passed into the darkness of death'. Odysseus the brave warrior shed a tear.

King Henry III of France (1575) was a devoted dog lover – perhaps a bit too devoted. He owned 2000 dogs, so it is perhaps just as well that he had several palaces. He liked to have at least 100 dogs within patting distance, and he went walkabout with 20 at a time.

In the thirteenth century, **Marco Polo** reported from China that Kublai Khan of Cathay had two *kivichi* or Masters of the Chase, each with 10,000 men assisting the Khan to command a total of 5000 dogs in tracking, hunting and killing wildlife. Marco Polo didn't mention how big the kennels must have been.

# Lord Byron

'Tis sweet to hear the watch-dog's honest bark
Bay deep-mouthed welcome as we draw near home.
'Tis sweet to know there is an eye will mark
Our coming – and look brighter when we come.

Lord Byron, *Don Juan*

In 1841, Scottish author Catherine Sinclair (in *A Month at Harrowgate*) quoted Lord Byron:

'Nobody need want a friend who can get a dog.'

Byron's sentiment kept turning up in various versions over the following century and beyond. A 1911 American newspaper advertisement in the Pets for Sale section advised: 'If You Want a Friend – Buy a Dog!' Following that, other classified advertisements used the same slogan, usually referring to dogs, but in at least one instance, to burglar alarms. By 1941 the line took on a new shape when American movie actor Frank Fay reportedly advised a French director newly arrived in Hollywood: 'If you're going to stay in this town and want a friend, go out and buy yourself a dog.'

In that other sphere of influence, Washington, President Harry S. Truman reputedly once announced that 'If you want a friend in Washington, get a dog.' This may have been apocryphal, however: there is scant evidence that Truman said it – and he didn't have a dog!

Lord Byron's dog **Boatswain** died in 1808 and was buried at Newstead Abbey. His epitaph reads:

> Near this spot are deposited the remains of one who possessed Beauty without Vanity, Strength without Insolence, Courage without Ferocity, and all the virtues of Man without his Vices. This praise, which would be unmeaning Flattery if inscribed over human ashes, is but a just tribute to the Memory of Boatswain, a Dog.

> The poor dog, in life the firmest friend,
> The first to welcome, foremost to defend,
> Whose honest heart is still his master's own,
> Who labours, fights, lives, breathes for him alone.

In the days before photography it was the custom for lovers to exchange a lock of their own hair. In his time, Byron had sent many of these to his various fans and lovers. But recent DNA analysis of over 100 samples sent by Byron shows that most of these came from a dog … in all probability, Boatswain.

'Hark, hark, the dogs do bark ...
The beggars are coming to town
Some in rags and some in jags
And one in a velvet gown.'

This English rhyme dates back several centuries and was sung by itinerant musicians, whose offerings frequently alluded to social conditions of the time and might even be classified as propaganda. Because the songs travelled with the musicians from district to district, subtle meanings in apparently innocent lyrics could enhance feelings of wider social discontent and even help to encourage uprisings. While it was common knowledge that dogs barked at the approach of strangers, the contrast between 'beggars' and those in velvet and 'jags' (deliberate slits or 'slashes' in fabric showing fancier material beneath) referred to the discontent among the poor and their resentment at the arrogance of the noble and wealthy. King Henry VIII's dissolution of the monasteries and the subsequent homelessness of monks, and the luxurious lifestyles of Elizabeth I and William III, are reputed to have incited crowds of the poor to sing 'Hark, hark, the dogs do bark' to them in the streets.

**Dog tired** is a familiar phrase, indicating that someone has reached the point of being too worn out to continue, and wishes simply to lie down without preliminaries or apologies of any kind, curl up and go to sleep – as a dog does.

**Let sleeping dogs lie** means to avoid trouble by remaining discreet, not attempting to make changes which could cause trouble. The expression has been in use since at least 1374, because Chaucer advises: 'It is not good a sleeping hound to wake'.

**Lie doggo** means to keep still, but not necessarily because one is tired or asleep. When a dog wishes to, it can become impressively motionless, lying low and quiet, with only the eyes flickering. Thus a person going into hiding or keeping quiet about something is like a dog – still, and giving out no clues. Adding the 'o' to the relevant noun somehow lifts the word 'dog' out of the ordinary (as in boy / boyo).

**Staffordshire** pottery makers took an interest when it became known that Queen Victoria loved spaniels – particularly her own Cavalier King Charles, 'Dash'. This is the reason for the proliferation of Staffordshire pottery spaniels from the mid-1800s. They did make other dog figurines – Dalmatians, poodles, pugs, pointers, foxhounds, sheepdogs, staghounds, setters and greyhounds – but they were less frequently seen.

**Pomerania** is a large region situated on the Baltic Sea between Germany and Poland. Pomerania is a Slavic word meaning 'by the sea' and has had that name for over a thousand years. One kind of dog from Pomerania was bred for very tough conditions, drawing sleds and herding sheep. The original Pomeranian dogs were quite big and impressive and were exported from Pomerania to be kept as pets for Mozart, Marie Antoinette and, eventually, Queen Victoria. Victoria liked small dogs, so breeders supplied her with their smallest progeny, which she occasionally put into dog shows and sometimes won. As a result, the breed not only became very popular among the British public but also grew smaller and smaller. But they retain the intelligence of their ancestry and are still popular pets.

Fraser Island off the east coast of Australia is the home of one of the purest strains of **dingo** (the Australian wild dog). Domestic dogs are banned on the island to avoid inter-breeding, as the Fraser Island dingoes are believed to represent an unbroken line back to the first domestic descendants of the wolf. They are therefore more closely related to the original dog species than any other. According to Chief Conservation officer Colin Lawton, the dingoes' ancestors were brought to Australia several thousand years ago by Asian seafarers. Descendants of those early canines can now be found throughout Australia, but those on Fraser Island (a heritage site) are 'pretty much the same as primitive dogs'.

In *The Beauty of Dogs*, Kenneth Bailey mentions an alternative view: that dingoes started out as domestic dogs which have gone back to a wild state.

**Organised hunting** of foxes by dogs was known in Britain as early as 1534. A century later, whole packs of dogs were being specifically trained to hunt foxes – a practice which continued for more than three hundred years. Then in 2000 Scotland banned fox-hunting, and in 2004 England and Wales followed suit. However, a version of the hunt still occurs, using fox-identical scent laid in areas and on tracks which real foxes might feasibly have frequented.

The **Basenji** hunting dog originated in the Congo and was familiar to the Pharaohs of ancient Egypt several thousand years BC. It arrived in Britain only in the late 1930s, and a few years after that in America. It is known as the 'barkless' dog, but the breed is not totally silent. The Basenji does a version of a growl and a snarl, and when happy makes a sort of chortling yodel. But it does not actually bark.

In 2002 the Japanese company Takara launched the **Bowlingual**, a device its makers claimed could 'translate' dog barks into recognisable speech. A small microphone attached to the dog's collar transmits the sound of any bark to a compact hand-held device (presumably in the owner's hand) containing a miniature computer. Inside it, several thousand pre-recorded dog barks have been stored in six categories: happy, sad, angry, needing attention, frustrated, and guarding. The computer compares the received bark to this database and identifies which category it most resembles. This is then displayed on a small screen, accompanied by an 'appropriate' phrase to match. Although described by its makers as a 'translator', the Bowlingual has more pragmatically been described as an 'emotion analyser'.

**His bark is worse than his bite**. This common phrase can be absolutely literal, in that a dog with a compelling basso bark accompanied by a display of great energy can, after a few moments' reflection, resolve into a wagging rag doll only waiting to be patted. In human terms, the phrase indicates that a scary persona, ominous behaviour or even verbal abuse may only be bluster and not serious aggression at all. The expression was in use at least as early as 1651, when George Herbert used it in his *Jacula Pudentum*.

**Why keep a dog and bark yourself?** This advice dates back as early as 1583 when it appeared in Brian Melbancke's novel *Philotimus*: 'It is small reason you should keep a dog, and bark yourself.' He was telling us that if you appoint someone for a particular job or purpose, it does not make sense to become too involved and start doing it yourself.

**Surgical de-barking** of dogs has several other names: devocalisation, vocal cordectomy and ventriculo-cordectomy. The operation involves removing tissue from the animal's vocal chords in order to reduce the volume of barking – or banish it completely. The process became illegal in Britain in 1992.

**Barking mad**. This phrase describing mad (or rabid) dogs has been around for many decades, but over time its meaning has softened a little. Someone described as 'barking mad' could be being pictured as just silly and irrational rather than wild and uncontrollable.

Prominent British animal psychologist Dr Roger Mugford runs the Animal Behaviour Centre in Surrey (he trained Princess Anne's dogs). In 2003 the *Economic Times* reported that Dr Mugford had invented a **wag-o-meter**, which was launched at the Wag and Bone Show at Ascot. The device is attached to the back of a dog, and has sensors which extend out onto the tail, where they measure the speed, direction and 'arc' of the wagging. Dr Mugford decreed that a wide horizontal wag indicated happiness. But beware if the tail goes straight up with just a tiny wag at the tip, because that means an attack is imminent. Whether these research results were groundbreaking is a moot point, but what wasn't explained was the significance of no wagging at all.

British television host Graham Norton introduced audiences to an invention he had been sent: a dog's tail for humans. Large and furry, the false tail was designed to be attached to a waist belt and contained a small, battery-operated, internal motor which could reposition the tail to fairly accurate manifestations of joy, sadness, excitement, doubt and anger. A limiting factor was that these reactions could only occur when the wearer pushed the appropriate button at the end of a not-very-discreet cable.

**'Tail between the legs'** is one of the easiest dog metaphors to identify with. There is no difficulty in picturing a dog with head down and tail limp, exhibiting guilt, humiliation or insecurity from every pore. A human might not adopt a drooping physical stance, but the similarity between the dog's emotions and the parallel state in a human is clear and inescapable. The term first appears in 1490 in a book by an Italian professor of surgery, Guido Lanfranchi, who described a hound with 'his tail bitwene hise leggis; his tunge hanging out.'

'**The tail wagging the dog**'. Abraham Lincoln was assassinated while watching a play called *Our American Cousin* by Tom Taylor. A character in that play, Lord Dundreary, frequently got common phrases muddled up, saying, for example: 'birds of a feather gather no moss' and 'a stitch in time never boils'. During the 1870s the saying that 'a dog being wagged by its tail' arose in America as an imitation of what Lord Dundreary might have said. It means, of course, that a supposedly minor entity with little discernible power is actually a controlling force in the larger organisation of which it is a part.

**Like a pup with two tails**. A dog's happy tail-wag is delightful to see, and one has the distinct impression that the dog enjoys doing it. So it is especially heart-warming to imagine that a dog blessed with two tails would be registering a double dose of happiness to all concerned, including itself.

**'Turnspit dogs'** in earlier times were not uncommon in the big houses of Britain, where they worked in the kitchen. And work they certainly did. Suspended near the fireplace was a wooden wheel enclosed in a circular box, attached to a spindle which turned the spit on which large roasts were cooked on the open fire. The 'turnspit dogs' were placed in the circular box and required to work it with their feet like a never-ending treadmill until the meat was cooked – which could take up to three hours. The dogs appointed to the task tended to be long-bodied and short-legged, and would be upbraided by the kitchen staff if they stopped treading the wheel.

In 1576, Dr John Caius, president of the College of Physicians and doctor to Mary I and Elizabeth I, published *Of Englishe Dogges: The Diuersitie, the Names, the Natures, and the Properties.* Included were his comments on 'turnspit dogs':

> There is comprehended under the curs of the coarsest kind a certain dog in kitchen service excellent. For when any meat is to be roasted, they go into a wheel, which they turn about with the weight of their bodies, so diligently look to their business, that no drudge nor scullion can do the feat more cunningly, whom the popular sort hereupon term turnspits.

The Abergavenny Museum in Wales retains one of the old turnspit dog wheels on display.

Two turnspit dogs were usually assigned for duty, since after long hours of trotting to nowhere a dog could not be expected to maintain sufficient energy to repeat the same function effectively the following day. There are reports that the two dogs came to know which was 'their' day – and would hide. Some people believe this is the origin of the saying **'Every dog has his day'**.

## On the treadmill

On the same principal as turnspit dogs revolving a roast, the American company Sears Roebuck (slogan: 'Cheapest Supply House on Earth') offered a 'dog power' device for sale in 1897. It consisted of a small treadmill connected to any appliance which required turning, such as a butter churn, washing machine, corn grinder or even printing press. The dog was put onto the treadmill and encouraged to trot to nowhere *ad infinitum*, or at least until the butter was churned. The percentage of power produced by the trotting dog was relative to the weight of the animal. For jobs requiring more effort, a two-dog treadmill was also available. Sears Roebuck helpfully advised that if a dog didn't have the weight or stamina (and presumably also the inclination) to trot the treadmill, a pet goat or sheep could be used instead.

Sears' sales pitch included the line, 'If you keep a dog, make him work for a living', a sentiment no doubt shared by farmers who use dogs for herding sheep and guarding cattle. At least farm dogs have the satisfaction of seeing and understanding the success of their labours.

**A dog's life**. Dogs have not always been prized as friends or 'family members'. Historically they have sometimes been seen as pariahs and scavengers of the streets. Other dogs were regarded as useful for hunting but may have been given the crudest of shelters, surviving on food scraps from the master's table. During the 1500s the term 'dog's life' came into being in England, comparing anyone impoverished or living in drudgery with the life of a less than respected dog. Other classes of dogs did exist: companions to the wealthy; rural and snow dogs whose work was respected. But the curs, the strays and the scavengers appeared to live an unwelcome and miserable existence and their life was a struggle. So in 1542, when Erasmus wrote: 'The most parte of folks calleth it a miserable life, or a dogges life', he was referring to those on the dog-ladder's lower rungs. Fortunately many dogs now lead lives filled with joyful and active contentment.

**Work like a dog**. When they are not urban pets or strays, dogs often work for their living. Whatever the work is – and it could be on farms, at airports or in snow – these dogs often give a fine impression of *enjoying* what they do. This casts some doubt on the usual meaning of the phrase 'work like a dog', which somehow gives the impression of working under duress and for little reward. Doubtless this does happen sometimes, but watch a high-energy border collie skilfully rounding up a random flock of sheep, and you're watching sheer joy on four legs.

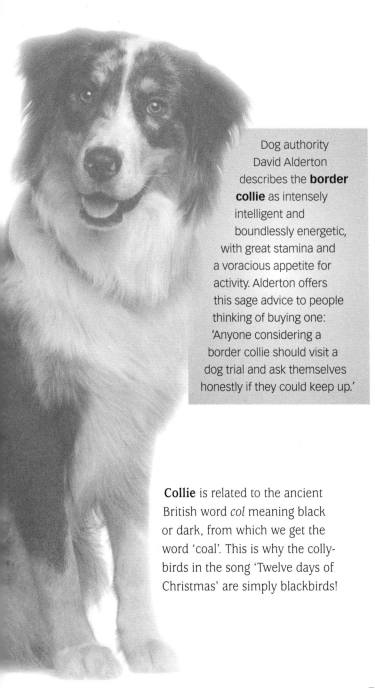

Dog authority David Alderton describes the **border collie** as intensely intelligent and boundlessly energetic, with great stamina and a voracious appetite for activity. Alderton offers this sage advice to people thinking of buying one: 'Anyone considering a border collie should visit a dog trial and ask themselves honestly if they could keep up.'

**Collie** is related to the ancient British word *col* meaning black or dark, from which we get the word 'coal'. This is why the colly-birds in the song 'Twelve days of Christmas' are simply blackbirds!

# Snow rescue dogs

To demonstrate the skill of Montana snow-guardian dogs in Yellowstone Park, actor Martin Clunes was filmed being deliberately buried in a cave of impacted snow. The dogs were held well out of sight while rangers traversed a wide snow-covered hillside to choose a locale well away from the base. There they built not one but three humps of snow, inside one of which Clunes crawled (equipped with a small radio transmitter which he could operate in avalanche conditions, just in case). The entrance was blocked with thick snow and the rangers tramped all around in random patterns, to lay confusing scent evidence, before trekking back to Search headquarters. Snow rescue dogs and other trailing dogs follow minute particles of human tissue or skin cells which have fallen to the ground. The dogs can also detect the faint smells which bodies emit, which tell them whether the person found is still alive or already dead. When the dog designated to 'rescue' Martin Clunes was released, true to form she capered purposefully over the wide-ranging area and, ignoring two of the humps, within minutes had zeroed in on the one containing Clunes. Inside, he saw the darkness begin to lighten, and the snow above him start to recede as he became aware of paw-scrabbling and joyous yapping. While no avalanche had occurred for this demonstration, it is not difficult to imagine the relief these brilliant dogs would bring to someone trapped for real.

**Greyhound**. The meaning of the word 'hound' has not changed much since its early use in English (as *hund*). But the 'grey' part of the breed's name is more perplexing. It is generally believed to come from the Old English word *grig*, whose exact meaning is unclear – except that it doesn't appear to have anything to do with colour. During the medieval period, the English aristocracy encouraged the breeding of greyhounds in a variety of colours. A slew of conjecture about what *grig* could have signified in the breed's original name has reached no conclusion. The name remains a mystery.

The greyhound is the only dog mentioned by name in the Bible – depending on which version you have. The King James version (1611) names the greyhound as one of the 'four things stately' in Proverbs 30:31. However, some later scholars have translated the original Hebrew as 'strutting rooster' rather than greyhound.

**'Like a dog with a bone'**. A dog with a bone is (a) happy, (b) somewhat guarded and (c) busy. The bone usually has its full and determined attention. An old Dutch proverb asserts: 'A dog with a bone has no friends.' Both the phrase and the proverb describe someone who has an agenda which they are reluctant to let go.

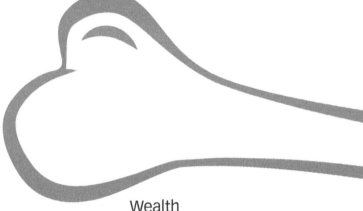

## Wealth

When she died in 1991, German-born Countess Karlotta Liebenstein left her entire fortune to her pet German shepherd, Gunther III. The amount she left was sufficiently eye-watering to be reported confusingly in amounts ranging from $106 million to $145 million. A stipulation was that the capital must eventually be passed on to Gunther's heir. When the time came for Gunther IV to take over, the fortune had accumulated to an impressive – and generally agreed – $372 million. In July 2000, the BBC reported that Gunther IV had bought Madonna's palatial mansion in Miami (besides already owning villas in Italy and the Bahamas). He would sleep in Madonna's former bedroom and the rest of the house would be used for 'filming and fashion shows'.

Another wealthy woman caused a stir over a dog in 2009 – but this time she was still alive. The *New York Post* reported that a wealthy Chinese woman, who already owned a fairly rare Tibetan collie, was visiting the Qinghai province and saw another one – 18 months old and 80 cms (31 inches) high. She felt she had to have this one too, so bought it for a reported cost of $585,000 – at that time thought to be the highest price ever paid for a dog. According to local reports, the dog's travel and arrival in his new province was in red carpet style: a throng gathered to see a motorcade of 30 vehicles collect him from Xi'an airport and deliver him to Mrs Wang's home.

**'Lucky dog'**. The term certainly applied to Gunther – but it is not specific to dogs. It is common to call someone a lucky *something* – the speaker can supply their own noun of choice. Among friends this is usually something slightly unexpected in terms of being lucky, such as 'devil' or 'swine' – but in a tone which makes it clear that the noun is a deliberate and mildly affectionate joke.

# Clones

Most people have heard of Dolly, the cloned sheep, but less well known is Snuppy, the cloned dog. In August 2005 the BBC carried a report that scientists in South Korea had produced the first dog clone. Researchers said that the new Afghan hound Snuppy was still doing well after 16 weeks. Snuppy (an abbreviation of Seoul National University puppy) was made from a cell taken from the ear of a three-year-old male Afghan hound.

Other animals have been successfully cloned, but cloning dogs is known to be difficult. The South Korean team made over 1000 embryo transfers into 123 recipients (surrogate 'mothers') but of these, only Snuppy remained alive and well. His birth generated moral concerns in some quarters, condemning genetic manipulation. A spokesman for the Kennel Club (committed to promoting the improvement of dogs) asked, 'Will these cloned dogs end up being used in a laboratory?'

The cloning of a particular dog made a couple in Florida very happy during 2009 – at a price. After their beloved Labrador Lancelot died, they heard that a cloning attempt could be made in Korea. The cost could hardly be called modest, but Edgar and Nina Otto were able to afford it. They agreed to the deal, and an egg containing DNA from their original Lancelot was transferred into a bitch in Korea. After the pup was born and reached a level of independence, he was flown to Miami to meet his 'father's' family, to great rejoicing.

He was immediately named Encore – so exact was his likeness to the late departed. Encore appeared on the 'Today' television show with his new family, who were asked if they felt the expense had been justified. Edgar Otto said, 'We feel it was worth it.' The total cost of acquiring Lancelot's clone was $155,000.

Disney star **Pluto** first appeared in 1930 as a bloodhound chasing Mickey Mouse. But cartoon land is liberal about relationships, and Pluto eventually became Mickey's pet and best pal. He's not the only dog in the Disney coterie of mouse-plus-dog anthropomorphism. There's an unfriendly bulldog called Butch, a Pekingese called Fifi, and Dinah the dachshund with the fluttering lashes … not to mention Pluto's quintuplet pups.

Pluto acquired an unexpected association with World War Two. In order to supply fuel to Allied armed forces on the continent of Europe, Britain built a secret pipeline across (and beneath) the English Channel. Millions of gallons were pumped through it daily from a land-based station disguised as an ice cream factory. Secrecy was preserved by giving the project the code name PLUTO: Pipe Line Under The Ocean.

Similarly, in peacetime:

**BIRDDOG** is an acronym for Basic Investigation of Remotely Detectable Deposits of Oil and Gas (an American Geological survey).

**FIDO** is the coin collectors' description of minted coins with irregularities: Freaks, Irregulars, Defects, Oddities.

**PAWS** is shorthand for Phased Array Warning System: US space surveillance tracking missiles and other things.

> ***National Geographic*** worked out that if humans varied as much in height as the various breeds of dogs do, the tallest human would tower at 31 feet (9.45 metres) and the shortest would be a modest two feet tall (61 cms).

## Clothes

In one of their television programmes, British style gurus Trinny and Susannah attempted to offer dress advice to dog-owners, especially when out walking their pets. Their decrees resulted in many dog-owners taking to blogs and forums with withering scorn. It was pointed out, in no uncertain terms, that clothes worn for dog-walking needed to be practical, and that protection from mud, hairs, grass stains, wind, cold and wet-shaking took precedence over style. Moreover, tracksuit bottoms, waterproof boots and hooded fleece jackets with pockets for leads, poo-bags and tennis balls were much more functional than stilettos and a mini-skirt. One dog-lover wrote that 'The words "dog-walking" and "chic" are mutually exclusive.' Fashion was firmly put in its place, and 'after all, the dogs don't care what we look like.'

# Neuticles

The American veterinary industry has given our language a new word: **neuticles**. The word has arisen from the universally common practice by which, for various reasons, some animals are castrated. Nothing new about that – but has your animal suffered an emotional 'post-neutering trauma'? An advertising campaign in America has already persuaded over 100,000 pet owners that a castrated animal needs to be fitted with 'testicle prostheses', otherwise known as neuticles. Owners are assured that their pet 'wants to look the same as he did before neutering' – and that his sense of self-esteem must not be overlooked. 'Consider your pet's male pride,' announces the firm which manufactures neuticles. 'Protect his masculinity – he will not want to be regarded by other dogs as a second-class citizen. Fitted with neuticles, he will not only look right, but will also feel right – as if nothing has changed.'

The manufacturers have licensed a particular mix of silicone with a 'natural' texture, which can match your pet's departed accessories in size, weight and feel. Initially five different sizes were available. But neuticles for dogs have been such a success that the range has been extended to testicle prostheses for cats, bulls and horses! Prices start at $60 a pair and rise to a luxury set costing $130 'plus implantation fee'. And should your pet's fragile self-esteem include possible embarrassment at the thought of a 'neutering scar', a pricey anti-scarring gel treatment will ensure that only his vet knows for sure.

Prosthetic testicular 'substitutes' have long been available for adult men who have developed testicular cancer requiring excision. And for exactly the reasons outlined above: self-esteem, a feeling of normality and no puzzled looks from team-mates in the shower room. But it is probably more difficult to accept that the same social and personal concerns affect the psyche of dogs, cats, bulls and horses. However, if you decide that neutering will cause your pet to be appearance-disadvantaged (as well as disadvantaged in the more obvious way), then for $60 upwards 'plus implantation fee' a pair of neuticles will take care of the situation.

**(The) black dog (walked over him)**. Through no fault of their own, perfectly innocent black dogs have sometimes had unwelcome imagery thrust upon them – even as far as claiming a black dog is really the devil in disguise. In *c*.50 BC the Roman poet and satirist Horace used the image of a black dog as a bad omen, and by the 1700s it was established in English as a synonym for depression, with a period of severe depression being described as a visit from a black dog. Samuel Johnson referred to it in this way, as did Sir Walter Scott and Robert Louis Stevenson. When Winston Churchill later acknowledged his own periods of depression, writers referred to it as his 'black dog', though there is scant reliable evidence that Churchill ever said it himself.

Goethe's *Faust* (1808) features an early example of the devil appearing in the form of a black dog. Dr Faust has failed to invoke the magic to give him infinite knowledge, so he gloomily goes out to listen to some Easter celebrations. On the way home, a black dog joins him, but it behaves rather oddly and follows him right into his study. The dog transforms into Mephistopheles and suggests an evil bargain: that he will grant Faust everything he desires on Earth in return for his soul after death.

**The Baskerville hound**. For centuries, inhabitants of various areas of England have told tales about a large, terrifying killer dog, sometimes headless, or with saucer-size, malevolent, flaming eyes (or just one eye). These legendary figures were sometimes reported to be dogs as large as a calf. They were known in different regions as Black Shuck, the Barghest, Skriker, Gytrash or the Yeth Hound.

Squire Richard Cabell was the (real) wicked Lord of the Manor in Brook, near Buckfastleigh in Devon, and lived in Brook Manor. A legend arose that on the night he died in 1677, a pack of ghostly black hounds galloped across Dartmoor breathing flames and smoke, ending up at Brook Manor, howling. A local belief that the squire's ghost and the dogs continued to roam long after his death led to the building of walls around the perimeter of his grave, topped with a massively heavy slab roof to contain the squire's spirit and his howling companions. It can still be seen intact amid the ruins of Holy Trinity Church in Buckfastleigh. Imaginative souls continue to report that a red glow can sometimes be seen coming through the grave walls' iron bars – and suspicious folk are warned not to put their finger between the bars in case the spirit hounds bite them.

It is believed that Sir Arthur Conan Doyle drew on the legend of Squire Cabell and his hell hounds when he wrote *The Hound of the Baskervilles* in 1901.

**Punch and Judy** puppet shows, usually performed in a tall narrow booth with an open stage at the top, are based on the ancient Italian comedy figure Pulcinella. The British version has been performed since 1662. The story customarily involves a lot of knockabout farce, with considerable variation depending on current affairs and the location of the performance. Mr Punch and his wife Judy are joined by other characters: a policeman, a baby, a doctor, a crocodile, some sausages (important to the story – thus counted as a character), and Toby the dog (important to the sausages). Toby always wears a distinctive frilled collar adorned with little bells. Although he and Mr Punch share scenes and communicate, credibility is not stretched so far as to require Toby to speak dialogue. He only says 'Bow wow' and 'Arrrrr' (before biting Mr Punch on the nose).

The fictional terrier **Toto** was created in 1900 as the pet of Dorothy Gale in Frank Baum's book about the Wizard of Oz. In the later movie starring Judy Garland, Toto, although referred to as male, was played by a female Cairn terrier called Terry. One of movie history's most memorable lines is spoken to the terrier when Judy Garland, as Dorothy, is somewhat alarmed at the strange land in which she has found herself and says: 'Toto – I have a feeling we're not in Kansas any more.'

*Wizard* wasn't Terry's only movie; she appeared in others with Shirley Temple, Joan Crawford, Norma Shearer and Spencer Tracy. But one of the dog's most indelible moments never appeared on screen: on the day movie star Clark Gable came to meet her, she leapt up and knocked out his false teeth.

**Dog carts** are exactly what the name suggests: carts pulled by dogs. Eskimos, native Americans, Russians and much of the rest of the world used dog power for hauling vehicles of varying size (with varying numbers of dogs). In arctic regions they still do. But solo dog carts were in common use, both in times of war and peace, particularly when carrying provisions for sale or delivery such as bread, milk and meat. There was no cruelty involved: the trader needed the dog, so the dog was kept comfortable and healthy. It has been estimated that at the start of the twentieth century, 300,000 dog-hauled carts were in use in Belgium alone – indeed, they may be seen in many Belgian paintings and postcards of the era. Some countries now ban the use of dogs attached to carts. The city of London banned them in 1839, and a bill was introduced into the British Parliament in 1841 to ban the use of dog carts throughout the kingdom.

**Borzoi** is a version of the Russian word *borzaya* which translates as 'quick dog'.

**Samoyed** is a Siberian breed named after the Samoyedic people of the Russian arctic coast.

In 2011 an abandoned chihuahua with a severe skin disease was taken in by the Battersea Dogs Home in London. A young woman working there took a liking to the little one, and as the dog healed, she took her to some training sessions for border collies. The chihuahua appeared interested in what was happening, and one day took to the training ring herself. To everyone's amazement the tiny chihuahua (2.1 pounds / 1 kilogram) instantly took charge and proved to be a highly efficient musterer – of animals six times taller than herself. Fox News reported: 'She is now capable of showing full-grown sheep who is boss.' Her minder, Ali Taylor, was not altogether surprised. She said: 'Dogs can do amazing things.'

**Chihuahuas** are named after the Free and Sovereign State of Chihuahua within the 32 Federal Entities of Mexico.

The famous dog trainer **Barbara Woodhouse** gave some cautionary advice to potential dog owners. In *The Beauty of Dogs* she drew attention to the fact that in choosing a family pet, the length of its hair should be an influencing factor:

Mothers can become very annoyed at the amount of hair left around the house and on children's clothing, especially when the dog is casting its coat, which some dogs do perpetually. They may also object to having to groom dogs such as Old English Sheep dogs or Afghans, who are liable to bring an enormous amount of mud into the house if not dried properly.

**Dalmatia** is a region in the former Yugoslavia which now lies in modern Croatia. Dalmatian dogs didn't necessarily originate there, but were named by the English who took them back home and employed them as carriage dogs – running beside the carriages of fashionable ladies (sometimes between the wheels!) and warding off interference from other dogs. They can run up to 30 miles (42 kms) in a day.

The breed seems to have an affinity with horses and was often attached to the firehouse in the days of horse-drawn fire wagons. Since every firehouse had a set of fast horses to pull the pumper, it became common for each group of fire-fighters to keep a Dalmatian in the firehouse to guard the firehouse and horses. When the alarm sounded, the Dalmatian led the way for the horse-drawn pumper. Thus the Dalmatian became the fire-fighters' companion and a symbol of the fire service. Dalmatians are still found in some firehouses in England, Canada and the United States.

**Pongo and Perdita** are the cartoon stars in the famous animated Disney movie, *101 Dalmatians*. Pongo has 72 spots, Perdita has 68 and each of the puppies has 32.

# The Cruelty to Animals Act

The Cruelty to Animals Act (1835), which outlawed animal cruelty in Britain, legally put an end to bull-baiting and bear-baiting, but didn't include any protection for rats. Consequently there grew the sport of 'ratting', whereby captured rats were released alive into a pit and dogs released to kill as many as they could within a prescribed number of minutes. Bets were placed, and the dog which achieved the highest number of corpses won (or rather his owner did). At one time London was reputed to have 70 rat pits. The most famous rat-killer was a Manchester terrier called Billy. The October 1822 *Sporting Magazine* reported that Billy presented a lively audience with a dramatic display:

> The dog BILLY, of rat-killing notoriety, on the evening of the 13th instant, again exhibited his surprising dexterity; he was wagered to kill one hundred rats within twelve minutes; but six minutes and twenty-five seconds only elapsed, when every rat lay stretched on the gory plain, without the least symptom of life appearing. Billy was decorated with a silver collar, and a number of ribband bows, and was led off amidst the applauses of the persons assembled.

Although Billy was blind in one eye (having been bitten there by a rat when he was learning his craft) he clearly had the x-factor which makes a celebrity. By popular demand, he continued into his old age, when he had only two teeth. At one point in his career Billy's killing rate was 3.3 seconds per rat. Forty years later Billy's record was eclipsed by a black-and-tan bull terrier called Jacko, which in 1862 was reported by the *Sporting Chronicle Annual* to have a killing record of 2.7 seconds per rat – quicker than Billy by a difference of 0.6 of a second.

In 1666, after he'd been to a **bull-baiting**, the famous diarist Samuel Pepys wrote that the event was a 'rude and nasty pleasure'. Bull-baiting had been practised in England for centuries, often as an entertainment on the village green. A tethered bull was ritually tormented by tenacious bulldogs bred especially for the task. Thought to have originated from mastiff stock, through selective breeding bulldogs developed a jaw-clamp further forward than their nostrils, so they could still breathe after chomping onto a bull. As well, their face was encouraged to furrow with loose skin wrinkles, so any blood arising from the chomping would be channeled away from their eyes.

Bull-baiting became illegal in 1835, and the bulldog, which was not necessarily an aggressive dog at all (in non-combatant situations), became a well-loved symbol of British strength and reliability.

**King Charles spaniels** were so called because they were the favourite dog of King Charles II of England. Samuel Pepys recorded that the king loved dogs so much that he attended meetings of state with a dog in his arms. In Pepys's opinion the king derived more pleasure from his dogs than from his ministers.

The Cavalier King Charles is a more recent breed, equally attractive but significantly larger.

A Springer spaniel called Bob stood for British Parliament in 1982, representing 'The Monster Raving Loony Barking Mad Dog Party'. He was owned by David Sutch, better known as 'Screaming Lord Sutch'. The spaniel was not elected.

# Dog v Pope

It is possible that the history of Britain – and ultimately the entire structure of the Anglican and Episcopalian church – hinged on the behaviour of one spaniel. In 1530, King Henry VIII's wife Katherine of Aragon had not produced a male heir, and he was anxious to discard her in favour of the younger Anne Boleyn. But it was not easy to annul his Catholic marriage. Henry sent the Archbishop of Canterbury, Dr Thomas Cranmer, and Anne Boleyn's father, Lord Wiltshire, to meet Pope Clement V1 and put the King's case for annulment to the pontiff. Lord Wiltshire took along his pet spaniel, which accompanied him for the audience with the Pope.

According to Elizabethan historian John Foxe, the British gentlemen walked up to the Pope, who was sitting high and dressed in rich apparel. In accordance with the protocol he himself had devised, the Pope extended his foot to be kissed. Lord Wiltshire's dog apparently interpreted this sudden emergence of a leg as a possible danger to his master. Foxe writes:

> The spaniel, when the bishop extended his foot to be kissed, no man regarding the same, straight-way (as though he had been of purpose appointed thereunto) went directly to the pope's feet, and not only kissed the same unmannerly with his mouth, but, as some plainly reported and affirmed, took fast with his

mouth the great toe of the pope, so that he in haste pulled in his glorious feet from the spaniel.

The Pope showed no support for annulling the marriage of the Henry VIII. Henry therefore created the Church of England, appointed himself head of it and annulled his own marriage. Would events have unfolded differently had the spaniel not intervened and bitten the Pope's big toe?

There were dog passengers on the **Titanic**, but history doesn't record the exact number. Dogs weren't documented as meticulously as passengers. The fare for a dog was the same as a child – half the normal fare – so it was mainly wealthy first-class passengers who were accompanied by their pets. The larger dogs were kept in kennels below decks, the smaller lived in their owners' cabins. Walter Lord's *A Night to Remember* recounts that 'even the passengers' dogs were glamorous'. Millionaire John Joseph Astor was accompanied by his Airedale, Kitty, publisher Henry Harper took his prize Pekingese, and banker Robert Daniel had a champion bulldog.

Three small dogs are known to have survived the sinking: Mr Harper's Pekingese in lifeboat 3; a Pomeranian in lifeboat 6 with Elizabeth Barrett Rothschild; and another Pomeranian in lifeboat 7 with Miss Margaret Hays. All three owners were able to take their pets because there was room in the lifeboats – before things became desperate.

On 21 April 1912, the *New York Herald* reported that another dog, a big Newfoundland, had survived. After three hours in freezing water, his anguished barking alerted the captain of the *Carpathia* that another lifeboat was nearby. Unfortunately no rescued passengers ever verified the story, and there was disbelief that any dog – even a Newfoundland – could survive three hours in freezing waters and still be active. But the legend lives on.

Only two dogs are known to have sailed from England in the **Mayflower** with the Pilgrim Fathers to North America. A detailed account of the journey published in 1622, *Mourt's Relation* by Edward Winslow and William Bradford, stated: 'John Goodman and Peter Brown having a great Maftiffe bitch with them and a little Spanell.' Apart from the mastiff and the spaniel, no other dog appears in the account of the emigrants.

The word **spaniel** comes from Latin *hispaniolus*, meaning 'Spanish', which in French became *espaigneul*, meaning 'Spanish dog', acknowledging the dogs' historic connection to hunting in Spain, where it is believed to have originated. (Some take a different view and believe that the breed originated in China and was later introduced to southern Europe.)

Springer spaniels were so named for their ability to 'spring' or 'flush' game birds into the air. That same skill – flushing out game – is sometimes known as 'cocking', which may have been a factor in naming the breed now known as cocker spaniels. But these dogs also hunted wading birds and were highly regarded for their skill in hunting woodcocks, so this may also account for their name.

Spaniels were certainly known in England by the late 1300s. Chaucer mentions one in *The Canterbury Tales* when he describes a plain woman searching for male company. She 'hankers for every man she may see, for like a spaniel she will leap on him.'

# St Hubert

St Hubert is the patron saint of hunters, opticians, mathematicians, metal-workers, smelters, archers, forest workers – and dogs. The *Wordsworth Dictionary of Saints* also lists St Hubert as the saint to be invoked against rabies and hydrophobia. Historically this is based on rather slim information – a combination of myths and legends makes up most of what we know of Hubert. He is believed to have been the son of the Duke of Guienne and was a profligate, a party-goer and a keen huntsman. He even went hunting on Good Friday – and legend tells that a stag appeared before him bearing a flaming cross between its antlers and speaking in a voice which advised him to change his ways. Impressed by this (who wouldn't be?) he did change his ways and eventually became a Christian bishop.

No specific connection with dogs was ever verified, apart from their association with hunting, which he loved. Nevertheless, after his death two popular beliefs arose in Belgium and France that anyone suffering from a rabies bite could be cured by using an object associated with Hubert. Specifically, either a metal rod called Hubert's Key could be heated and placed on the location of the bite, or a small cut could be made in the forehead, into which was placed a thread taken from the late Hubert's cloak – the one he said had been given to him by the Virgin Mary. The success rate of either treatment has not been recorded.

Three hundred years after Hubert died, a breed of hunting dog arose from the monastery named after him. But the **St Hubert hound** had a rather patchy reception among hunters, and in spite of its ability to track by scent, the breed began to diminish in numbers, eventually to the point of invisibility. When a resurgence of interest in scenting dogs came about, the breeding strain of the St Hubert hound became one contributor to a carefully bred newcomer. This became known as a bloodhound, which in some places is still known as a St Hubert hound.

A real dog played a crucial role on stage in the 1814 French play **Le Chien de Montargis**. The dog is seen to witness the murder of his master (as does the audience) and sets out to provide the authorities with clues to identify the murderers. The play was staged with great success throughout Europe, and an English version, *Murder in the Wood*, played 1100 performances in England.

In Shakespeare's *Much Ado About Nothing* the character of **Dogberry** is a comical rustic constable. But his name has less to do with actual dogs than a common English shrub known as dogwood. The Elizabethan use of the word 'berry' refers to fish roe and builds an implicit verbal joke into the name, since to the Elizabethan ear Dogberry somehow suggests 'dog-roe' – an absurdity which fits perfectly with the character's bumbling incompetence.

The only dog character to appear in a play by Shakespeare is **Crab**, in *The Two Gentlemen of Verona*. Launce delivers the dog as a gift to Silvia, and when Crab urinates on the floor, Launce loves the animal so dearly he claims it was he who urinated – and so takes a beating in place of Crab.

**Mrs Patrick Campbell** was one of the grandest of Britain's *grandes dames* of the theatre. G.B. Shaw wrote the role of Eliza Doolittle in *Pygmalion* for her. A devoted dog lover, she brooked no interference or criticism about taking one or two of her pets everywhere with her. On one occasion, clutching her pet while exiting a London taxi, she was confronted by the irate driver who complained that her dog had 'lost control' and left a mess. Mrs Campbell drew herself up, looked him in the eye and said firmly: 'I did it.' She then swept away.

On another occasion, while en route to perform in America, Mrs Campbell tried smuggling her dog through Customs by enfolding him inside the lavishly swathed cape she was wearing. 'Everything was going splendidly,' she later recounted, 'until my bosom barked.'

A dog's **sense of smell** is described by international veterinary surgeon David Taylor as literally 'one million times more sensitive than our own'. In his book *You and Your Dog*, he explains that a human's nose is equipped with an olfactory sensing area of about three square centimetres. The same facility inside the muzzle of an average dog is 130 square centimetres. Its surface area is achieved by the sensitive tissue being folded into ripples which create 'trapping areas' for smelled information to react with densely packed sensory cells. Additionally, a dog has brain cells to recognise and identify 40 times as many scents as humans can. Dogs with a long nose have a more extended sensory area and tend to be super-efficient sniffers, while short, blunt-nosed dogs are slightly less capable.

Dogs need to sniff the ground; it's how they keep abreast of current events. The ground is a giant dog newspaper, containing all kinds of late-breaking dog news items, which, if they are especially urgent, are often continued into the next yard.
*Dave Barry*

Dog authority and historian **Cecil Wimhurst** reminds us how a dog's ability to identify scents is so acute:

> Scent is in the minute particles of matter which are deposited all the time by every living creature, whether moving or still, and is quite out of their control. Scent is left on grass, hard roads, plants or trees and on snow and ice. It will be deposited on water but will be moved swiftly away by the current. It can be carried by the wind and hang in the air so that a hound can follow it breast high.
>
> A damp atmosphere is favourable to scent, but a slight wind on a dry day will quickly cause it to evaporate and in a strong wind it will dissipate very quickly indeed. A scent over seven hours old is stale, although a bloodhound has been known successfully to complete a trail many hours older.

**Male dogs** lift their leg to urinate onto a surface, preferably vertical, to mark the territory. The deposit is at approximately nose-height for other dogs. Besides the urine performing its usual biological function, dog urine contains mineral traces and salts with scents which give important dog information to passing sniffers. The scent can tell the sniffer many things, including the health of the dog which left the deposit, and his size (judged by how high the deposit has been placed).

# Search-and-rescue

Dogs can be invaluable in search-and-rescue, and can assist in ascertaining if fire damage was deliberately caused (by seeking the presence of hydrocarbons). After familiarisation, they can also detect allergens (such as peanuts in food) and alert people for whom such things are dangerous. By the process known as biodetection, dogs can be trained to recognise the very slight odour caused by chemical matter in the early stages of various cancers: breast, bowel, uterine, bladder, prostate, lung and melanoma. With their fine scent-analysis powers, they can detect when a diabetes-prone person's blood-sugar level is becoming dangerously low. They can even sense when a seizure of some sort (such as epilepsy) is about to happen – and can bark for help and paw the person towards a safer place.

They can be trained to find truffles, locate termites in buildings and recognise the presence of alien bugs before they become established beyond control (for example, in vineyards).Their impressive ability to seek and identify scents plays a significant role in the law-and-order battle against illegal drugs. Sniffer dogs on searching missions or at airports can identify seeds, vegetation and forbidden fruits with ease and can detect drugs even when packed tightly amid mothballs. According to an official, a dog can 'screen people faster than an X-ray machine'.

Of the words any householder or hotel proprietor doesn't want to hear, **bed bugs** would be high on the list. These tiny pests are unwelcome, unpleasant, unhygienic and, if they become established, difficult to find and eradicate. The University of Kentucky (among others) has warned that the incidence of bed bugs is on the rise around the world. However, help is at hand. An extermination firm in Canada has succeeded in training the astonishing sensitivity of dogs' smell to sniff out the presence of bed bugs. Taken into a room, a dog can reveal in a few moments if bed bugs are present, and if so, will immediately zero in on where they are hiding.

In Italy, dogs have become expert **money-sniffers.** European Union regulations state that sums of 10,000 Euros or more must be declared when entering or leaving the EU. Duty must be paid on any amount above that, and if money is found not to have been declared, there are heavy fines and jail sentences. Italians flying to neighbouring Switzerland are actually leaving the EU (Switzerland is not a member), so the 10,000 Euros rule applies. Italians hoping to deposit larger amounts in Swiss banks are up against Italy's airport sniffer dogs. Concealing banknotes in underwear or hollowed-out leather luggage, disguising it amidst coffee or chilli, or even meticulously inserting it into cigarettes will not fool the expert canine nose. Incredibly, the dogs allow those passengers carrying only the allowable 10,000 Euros to pass unhindered, and only detain those who try to sneak through with more.

Dogs 'sweat' all over their bodies, though not so much for heat regulation, as is the case with humans. Their body sweat is tuned to give out secretions which identify them to other dogs. Humans tend to recognise what could be called a general **'doggy smell'**, but to a dog every member of the species has a different smell. Their 'sweat,' their urine and the tiny secretions from their anal glands leave messages for brethren, paramours and enemies. The underside of a dog's paws also sweats, but it is a kind of emollient, mainly to keep the paw surface soft, for without it constant friction between paw and terrain could damage the paw pad's surface. Unusually, the Mexican hairless dog does perspire through its skin, and seldom pants.

After defecating, a dog will often scratch the ground behind. This is to convey information by leaving a 'marking scent' which comes from tiny glands between the toes.

According to tests done at the Institute for the Study of Animal Problems in Washington D.C., dogs and cats, like people, are either right-handed or left-handed; that is, they favour either their right or left paws.

**Dr Doolittle's** dog Jip not only had a supremely sensitive sense of smell; he could talk and report what he knew too. When he went to the front of the ship and smelt the wind he started muttering to himself:

'Tar; Spanish onions; kerosene oil; wet raincoats; crushed laurel-leaves; rubber burning; lace-curtains being washed – No, my mistake, lace-curtains hanging out to dry; and foxes – hundreds of 'em – cubs; and – '

'Can you really smell all those different things in this one wind?' asked the Doctor.

'Why, of course!' said Jip. 'And those are only a few of the easy smells – the strong ones. Any mongrel could smell those with a cold in the head. Wait now, and I'll tell you some of the harder scents that are coming on this wind – a few of the dainty ones.'

And Jip poked his nose straight into the air and identified –

'Bricks,' he whispered, very low – 'old yellow bricks, crumbling with age in a garden-wall; the sweet breath of young cows standing in a mountain-stream; the lead roof of a dove-cote – or perhaps a granary – with the mid-day sun on it; black kid gloves lying in a bureau-drawer of walnut-wood; a dusty road with a horses' drinking-trough beneath the sycamores; little mushrooms bursting through the rotting leaves …'

It is estimated that more than 200,000 dogs were used in **World War Two**, including canine sentries and watchdogs, scouting and patrol dogs, messengers, ambulance dogs and search and rescue dogs. They detected mines, undertook parachute jumps and were often able to warn of impending dangers – for example, before radar was fully developed they could sometimes sense approaching aircraft.

In the quest for victory, some dogs even gave up their lives. During the German invasion of Russia, attacks by Nazi armoured columns were stopped by 'kamikaze dogs'. Russians had previously trained the dogs to enter tanks and armoured vehicles for their food. When warned that enemy tanks were approaching, the dogs would be kept unfed. They would then have electronic mines strapped to their backs and released once the oncoming German tanks were in sight. In Japan, dogs were trained to pull little carts filled with explosives, which they would haul into enemy camps.

> In her book *Animals in War*, **Jilly Cooper** comments that mascots can cheer soldiers, but those in high command can feel isolated. In such circumstances, a favourite animal can become good company. In World War Two, General Eisenhower took his Scottie everywhere with him, and once admitted that the dog was the only living thing he could talk to who didn't want to discuss the war.

In 1928 **Al Jolson** sang 'Rainbow around my Shoulder' and summoned applause by calling: 'Hot diggity dog! Hot kitty! Hot pussycat! Didn't I tell you you'd love it?' Twenty-eight years later, Pat Boone's version of Jolson's catch-cry became the major hit, 'Hot Diggity Dog'.

All household dogs in Britain were in a vulnerable position after 1322. A Parliamentary Act was devised, decreeing that 'Distress shall be taken for the King's debts'. This law enabled any pets to be legally taken and impounded in order to pay off debts which the King (Edward II) might incur. The law remained untouched (and presumably enforceable) for 690 years. But in April 2012, the *Financial Times* reported that the British Law Commission had presented Parliament with a list of rather eccentric ancient laws (800 in total) which were past their use-by date and ready for repeal. So British dogs can now breathe easily.

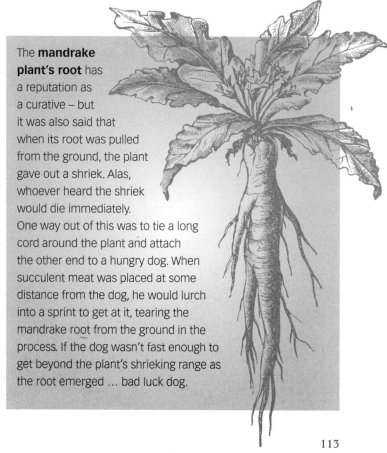

The **mandrake plant's root** has a reputation as a curative – but it was also said that when its root was pulled from the ground, the plant gave out a shriek. Alas, whoever heard the shriek would die immediately. One way out of this was to tie a long cord around the plant and attach the other end to a hungry dog. When succulent meat was placed at some distance from the dog, he would lurch into a sprint to get at it, tearing the mandrake root from the ground in the process. If the dog wasn't fast enough to get beyond the plant's shrieking range as the root emerged … bad luck dog.

Pet dogs often find **furniture** both useful and handy when they need something to chew on. Various commercial sprays have been designed to discourage this, especially if the furniture is leather (on which it is harder to conceal any chewing). One of these is a non-harmful but ill-tasting concoction called simply Bitter Bite.

One suggestion for preventing a dog from lying on an elegant couch is to keep underneath the couch a very long board onto which empty sardine tins have been nailed. This can be brought out and put in place when people are not using the couch. Apparently the dog will lie on it – very briefly and only once.

In Windsor Castle, the roof of the Chapel of St George features 76 large heraldic stone animals, known as **The Royal Beasts.** Each represents a heraldic symbol from kings and queens dating back to Tudor and Plantagenet times. They include a bull, falcon, lion, dragon, panther, swan, antelope – and one dog. This is the (rather plump) White Greyhound of Richmond, the symbol of Henry VII's father, the Earl of Richmond.

Two days before **Barbra Streisand** was scheduled to record her *Movie Songs* album, her pet bichon frise Sammy died, after seven years of companionship. The album included the song 'Smile', with melody composed by Charlie Chaplin for the 1936 movie *Modern Times*. In memory of her pet, Ms Streisand granted the rights to her 'Smile' track to the Humane Society of United States, whose 'Anthem of Spirit' it became. She said, 'The song brought me solace and if it does the same for others, that will be a very great reward.'

**In the doghouse**. In 1904 Sir James Barrie introduced the London theatregoing public to the fantasy figure of Peter Pan and the fictional Darling family. The family's children were looked after by Nana, a very domesticated Newfoundland (the character is believed to have been based on Barrie's own pet St Bernard, called Porthos).

The play portrays Mr Darling in an irritable mood one night, and instead of leaving Nana sleeping near the children, he ties her up to a kennel. Peter Pan arrives that night and lures the children away. When it is discovered that the children have gone, Mr Darling is in disgrace, since he had tied Nana up and thus prevented her from protecting the children. As punishment to himself, he takes up residence in Nana's kennel, so giving rise to the expression for being in disgrace: 'being in the doghouse'.

In March 1966, three months before the Jules Rimet Trophy would be awarded to the winner of the **FIFA World Cup**, the gold trophy was stolen from an exhibition in London's Westminster Hall. Seven days later a dog called Pickles found it, wrapped in newspaper and stuffed into a suburban hedge.

**Dog collar**. Apart from the obvious, this is also the vernacular name for the 'back to front' white collar worn by clerics in some religions. When in civvies, these church leaders sometimes cheat a little by carrying a narrow white plastic strip cut from the corner of an ice cream container, which can then be slipped into shirt-collar slots if required.

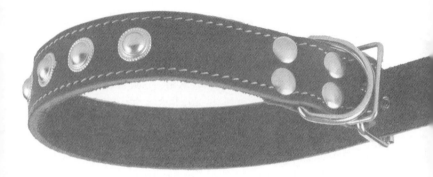

**'Put on the dog'** is to assume a style or image intended to suggest that one's status is more elevated than it is in fact. Less critically, it can also refer to dressing up in unfamiliar formality in order to take part in a specific event. In 1871 the expression was recorded in the United States in Lyman H. Bagg's *Four Years at Yale*: 'Dog – style, splurge. To put on dog is to make a flashy display, to cut a swell.' It may have arisen because formal dress for men required a high stiff collar, known colloquially as a 'dog collar' (see above), which was shortened to 'putting on the dog'. But the same era offers an alternative explanation for the phrase. After the Civil War, ladies of high society took to being accompanied by expensive lap dogs, the ownership of which became associated with 'advertising social prestige': they were 'putting on the dog'. At about the same time, the related adjective 'doggy' was a popular slang term meaning 'attractively stylish; costly; fancy'.

On hearing a woman preach in *c.*1763, **Dr Samuel Johnson** remarked: 'It was like a dog walking on its hind legs – it is not done well; but you are surprised to find it done at all.'

**'Done up like a dog's dinner'**. Dogs generally have little regard for 'silver service', so the usual image of a dog's dinner (or any other meal) is of enthusiastic consumption with little regard for order. How this applies to someone inappropriately overdressed (the usual meaning of 'a dog's dinner') is not quite clear, except perhaps that the dog's scattering of its leftovers could, at a pinch, be compared to someone heading out in an unusual excess of accessories.

**'See a man about a dog'** is commonly said to excuse oneself or to leave a meeting or a social gathering, sometimes when the speaker does not want to specify why (it may just be to go to the toilet). The earliest known use of the phrase was in the 1866 Dion Boucicault play *Flying Scud*, in which a character avoids a difficult situation by saying, 'Excuse me Mr Quail, I can't stop; I've got to see a man about a dog.' In a 1939 revival of the play on American radio, TIME magazine wrote that the phrase was the play's 'claim to fame'. During the Prohibition period in the United States, it was commonly used as a code for discreetly consuming alcohol.

An old proverb in print as early as 1490 gave some advice now considered unwise:

> A spaniel, a woman and a walnut tree,
> The more you beat them the better they be.

The rather unpleasant idea had first been suggested in Latin by Marxus Martialis, *c.* AD 100, in which he nominated a donkey rather than a spaniel:

> *Nux, asinus, mulier*
> *simili sunt lege*
> *Haec tria nil recte*
> *faciunt si verbera*
> *cessant.*

Aesop too advises the treatment to a donkey or an ass. The saying surfaced in different languages throughout Europe, but over the centuries the donkey was replaced by a spaniel, and then just a dog.

Tradition held that beating a walnut tree *did* improve its crop – breaking old twigs would encourage newer fruit-bearing growth. However, the University of California at Davis studied this ancient folklore and decreed it to be as inaccurate as the rest of the proverb.

*Rescued by Rover* in 1905 was the first movie starring a dog in the leading role. Filmed in Britain, the silent black-and-white short was such a success that 400 prints were sold and the movie had to be re-shot twice more because the negatives wore out. At the time, the name Rover was uncommon for a dog, but the success of the movie started a trend – and it became one of the most popular dog names.

**Rin Tin Tin** was one of two homeless German shepherd puppies found by an American serviceman in war-torn France during World War One. He took them back to the United States, where one died. The other became a major movie star, appearing in 26 films, earning life-saving monies for the Warner Bros studios. At his peak he received 10,000 fan letters a week, toured in vaudeville performances and even starred in radio shows, where he barked his own responses. When the dog died in 1932, American broadcasts interrupted their regular programmes to announce the sad demise. Rin Tin Tin was named after the woollen dolls which French children regarded as good luck charms.

In 1976 a spoof movie was made about a fictional dog which became a star: *Won Ton Ton – The Dog who Saved Hollywood*. The star was a dog called Augustus Von Schumacher.

**Goofy** is a very tall Disney cartoon dog born in 1932, a friend of both Mickey Mouse and Donald Duck – odd friends for a dog. But Goofy's likeable amiability was based on his being clumsy and rather dim, who would never harm anything, even a mouse.

The famous evolutionary scientist **Charles Darwin** greatly admired dogs. In *The Descent of Man* he wrote:

> Our domestic dogs are descended from wolves and jackals and though may not have gained in cunning, and may have lost in wariness and suspicion, yet they have progressed in certain moral qualities, such as affection, trust, worthiness, temper and probably in general intelligence.

Darwin put us to rights about the origin of species, and later the survival of the fittest, but he also had some nicely tuned observations about dogs:

> Dogs show what may fairly be called a sense of humour, as distinct from mere play; if a bit of stick or other such object be thrown to one, he will often carry it away for a short distance; and then squatting down with it on the ground close before him, will wait until his master comes quite close to take it away. The dog will then seize it and rush away in triumph, repeating the same manoeuvre, and evidently enjoying the practical joke.

And on varieties of barking:

> We have the bark of eagerness, as in the chase;
> that of anger, as well as growling; the yelp or howl
> of despair, as when shut up; the baying at night;
> the bark of joy, as when starting on a walk with
> his master; and the very distinct one of demand
> or supplication, as when wishing for a door or a
> window to be opened.

And a final thought from Charles Darwin: 'It is scarcely possible to doubt that the love of man has become instinctive in the dog.'

*Lady and the Tramp* in 1955 was the first animated feature film in widescreen CinemaScope. It tells the story of a gentle girl spaniel from a classy background whose friends are a neighbouring Scottish terrier and a bloodhound. Disturbed by a new and unwelcome development in her own household – the requirement to wear a muzzle – Lady sets out on an adventure, meeting up with a mutt named the Tramp who lives 'footloose and collar-free' with two chums: a Lhasa Apso and an English bulldog.

There is a Native American legend which recounts that when a human dies, their spirit must cross a bridge to enter the afterlife. Waiting at the head of the bridge is every animal the human encountered during their life. The animals discuss what they know about this human and their relationship with animals during their lifetime. Based on this, the animals decide who may continue over the bridge – and who must be turned back.

Leo Damrosch, the biographer of French writer and philosopher **Jean-Jacques Rousseau**, reports that Rousseau had a dog he called Duke. However, not wishing to embarrass his patron, the Duke of Luxembourg, he later changed the dog's name to Turk. Rumour had it that the duke was less offended by a dog being called Duke than by Rousseau's assumption that he could take a ducal title away!

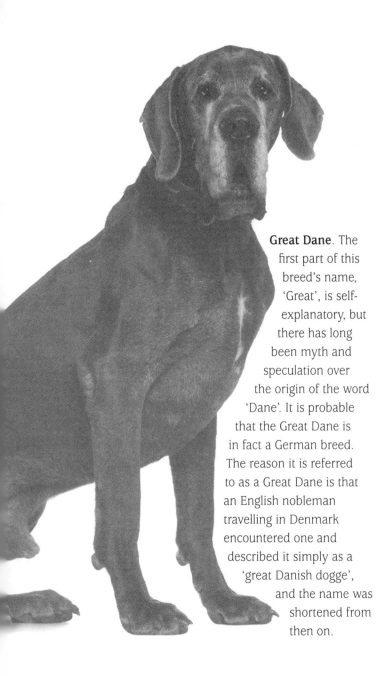

**Great Dane**. The first part of this breed's name, 'Great', is self-explanatory, but there has long been myth and speculation over the origin of the word 'Dane'. It is probable that the Great Dane is in fact a German breed. The reason it is referred to as a Great Dane is that an English nobleman travelling in Denmark encountered one and described it simply as a 'great Danish dogge', and the name was shortened from then on.

Mountaineering in the Ogwen Valley, Wales, proved too daunting in 2010 for Nero, a black Labrador. Anxious to accompany his owner, Nero mountain-tramped with her, but the surface proved so damaging to his paws that at 9100 metres the distressed animal could not keep going. The three-man Ogwen Valley rescue team went into action, and each took turns hoisting the 30-kilo dog onto their shoulders and walking down the difficult terrain until a colleague could take over. The Ogwen Valley rescue team had 144 call-outs that winter, but only one was for a dog.

**Labradors** are named after the coastal region of north-east Canada. Within the region is the island of Newfoundland, where the popular Labrador breed originated.

**Gordon setters** are named after the Dukes of Gordon.

**'The dog ate my homework.'** A colourful (and not always believable) excuse for not completing an essay, exercise or research within a required time. Writing analyst and educationist Christopher Simpson asserts that 12 January 1835 was the first known time the excuse was put forward, by a recalcitrant student called Henry Pennywhistle. A century after Pennywhistle, the author John Steinbeck reportedly found the first draft of his novel *Of Mice and Men* had been chewed up by his pet dog.

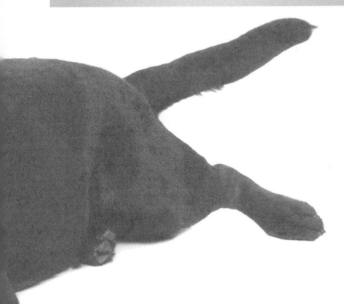

**Pliny the Elder**, the Roman author and naturalist who lived in the 1st century AD, wrote:

> Only dogs recognise their master, know when someone is a stranger, recognise their own names, and never forget the way to distant places. Next to man there is no living creature whose memory is so retentive.

# Pekingese

Pekingese (not Pekinese) was the favoured breed of the Imperial court when it ruled China. The court was part of the Forbidden City within Peking – hence the name of the breed. (Curiously, although the city is now known as Beijing, the dogs haven't yet been renamed Beijingese.) Breeders used the Pekingese to create dogs which looked as much as possible like the fancied lion.

One such was the **Shih-tzu**, meaning 'Lion Dog', which doesn't quite match the animal's small build and silky coat. The connection is with the ancient belief that Buddha was able to tame lions, which followed him like dogs. In early China, the legendary association of lions with Buddha led to the image of a lion becoming virtually a symbol of Buddhism, although few Chinese had ever seen a real lion. Nevertheless artists drew a version, and people were encouraged to breed dogs to resemble what became the 'traditional image' of a lion, whether the image was realistic or not. Outside China, in order to avoid any embarrassment when its name is said without sufficient separation of the two syllables, the Shih-tzu is sometimes known as the 'Chrysanthemum' dog.

**The Year of the Dog** occupies the 11th position in the 12-year cycle of the Chinese and Japanese zodiac. The Dog symbolises character traits such as loyalty, compatibility and kindness, frequently offers useful advice, always listens and lends a shoulder when necessary. Dogs often become deeply involved in others' lives and can sometimes be perceived as nosy. Ensuring others are happy is more important to the Dog than wealth, money or success. In addition, Dog people are determined individuals, always finishing what they start and always wanting to master a new subject before moving on. Dogs value friendships; they are loyal, honest, trustworthy and reliable, have strong morals and ethics and always keep secrets.

As the Chinese year is lunar, it does not automatically coincide with the Western calendar. It usually runs from mid-February to mid-January of the following year. You are probably a Dog if you were born in 1934, 1946, 1958, 1970, 1982, 1994, 2006, 2018, 2030.

It looks like a miniature hippopotamus with badly fitting pantyhose all over.
*Roger Caras describes the Chinese Shar-pei*

Since 1997, dogs have been able to attend a charming little chapel especially built for them in Vermont, USA. Designed in a traditional style, the chapel's peaked roof has a steeple topped by a figure of an 'angel dog' with wings, while at the main door is a life-size statue of a man leading his (ceramic) dog. Dogs attending the **Huneck Chapel** may be accompanied by humans, and the proceedings are carefully non-sectarian. A large elegant sign outside the chapel door announces: 'Welcome all creeds and all breeds. No dogmas allowed.'

**Dog Latin** describes the use of a spurious, inelegant quasi-Latin. Since it is far from accurate or grammatical, describing it as 'dog' Latin is thought to carry the connotation of 'mongrel'.

**Dogma**: A religious doctrine or system proclaimed by an ecclesiastical authority as true.

Etymologist Eric Partridge traces its use in English back through Indo-European to the Greek word *dokein*, meaning 'to believe', and from there through Latin to Old German. By the time it reached English the spelling had changed somewhat and become 'dogma' (with its adjective 'dogmatic'). The word has nothing to do with dogs.

In Greek mythology, **Actaeon the hunter** went to the forest one day with his 48 dogs and came across an unfamiliar glade, where in a calm pool the beautiful goddess Artemis was bathing naked. Actaeon gazed at her, relishing the sight, until the goddess noticed him watching her. She ordered him to remain silent for the rest of his life to ensure that any report of her nakedness was not repeated. If he ever spoke he would be transformed into a stag. Just then Actaeon heard his hunting dogs approaching, and without thinking he called out to them so they knew where he was – and was instantly transformed into a stag. The dogs arrived, did not recognise their master, and without hesitation all 48 of them immediately did what came naturally to them: they jumped on the stag and killed it.

In 1587 Robert Wingfield, through his connection to Lord Burleigh, witnessed the execution of **Mary Queen of Scots**. He reported that the Queen, robed elaborately, entered the place of execution led by the sheriff of the county, then kneeled and spoke a psalm in Latin. One of the two executioners held her down, while the other cut off her head and held it high.

Then one of the executioners spied her little dog – which had crept under her clothes, came forth from the dead corpse and laid between the severed head and corpse until forcibly removed and washed clean of the Queen's blood.

# Florence Nightingale

Florence Nightingale made a considerable mark in history. Her efforts and the respected profession she established are believed to have developed from her teenage encounter with an injured sheep dog. In *Lives of Girls who Became Famous*, Sarah Knowles Bolton recounts that when Florence was seventeen, a shepherd in her Derbyshire neighbourhood had a dog named Cap, which became a victim to passing hooligans throwing rocks at him. The attack was so violent that Cap was in great pain and could not walk. His distraught owner, Roger, decided that with such injuries Cap would not be able to do his work, so the right thing to do would be to put an end to his pain and his life. Roger went outside to find a piece of rope, preparing to hang the poor creature.

It so happened that while this was going on, Florence Nightingale was passing with the local vicar, and they called in to visit Roger. The dog Cap, which knew Florence, crawled towards her, his pain obvious. The vicar carefully examined the leg and came to the conclusion that it was not actually broken but very severely bruised. He and Florence found some old flannel, boiled water to make sure it was clean and applied compresses to the injury.

Roger returned to the house, holding a piece of rope and miserably preparing to do what he thought was right. Florence persuaded him to wait a day or two, promising to return to renew the compresses. Within two days, Cap

was on his feet, limping, but tail wagging, well on the way to recovery. The girl looked down at a dog clearly regaining its health: her first-ever patient.

The next day, still excited at her success, Florence was inspired to think she should proceed with learning to heal and nurture the sick as her mission. In doing so, she eventually became a legend.

**Adolf Hitler's** favourite dog was a German Shepherd called Blondi. Learning that capture by the Soviets was unavoidable, Hitler decided not to be taken alive. His secretary Traudl Junge later recounted that Hitler 'had begun to suspect that cyanide pills Himmler had supplied for Hitler's own suicide might be fake. So the Führer killed his own dog to make sure that his supply of suicide pills would work.' The cyanide pill killed Blondi immediately, so he knew the pills could bring about his own death – which they did.

**Abraham Lincoln's** pet dog did not accompany him to the White House after his master was elected President. Lincoln felt sure that clanging church bells and other city noises would be upsetting to the quiet-living canine. But one factor about the pet made a difference to the English language: Lincoln's dog was called Fido. So many people copied the President's choice of name that the word Fido (Latin for *faithful*) gradually became a generic term referring to any or all dogs.

**A TV commercial for dogs**. In February 2012 Britain saw its first TV commercial targeted directly at dogs. Dogs are often indifferent to television screens, but this Purina advertisement was cunningly devised. It was an engaging romp cleverly filmed and edited to show a group of dogs hijacking a delivery van filled with dog food. But its creators had taken into account the fact that sounds above 17,000 Hertz, which are not audible to humans, can alert dogs to pay attention. Hence there was a soundtrack to the commercial, which in itself made perfect sense to viewers, with music and expressions of human dismay (as a truck rolled into the distance 'driven' by dogs). However, there were additional doglike noises at a pitch which humans cannot hear, causing a reaction in household pets which owners were expected to interpret as dogs wanting the advertised food. The following day, the *Daily Telegraph* reviewed the commercial's debut and remarked somewhat cynically: 'Animals are the new marketing frontier.'

> **Poodles** originate from Germany and were named after the word *pudeln*: to splash in water. Their coats are very thick, which could slow them down in thick undergrowth or water, so much of the pelt was shaved lower, except for vulnerable areas like hindquarters and joints where the thick coat was retained to keep cold and dampness out and prevent rheumatism. Hunters customarily tied a ribbon of their identifiable colour into the topknot to help tell their own dogs from someone else's.

**Winston Churchill**, although identified with the bulldog, actually liked poodles. The Churchill family poodle Rufus ate in the dining room on a cloth laid on the Persian carpet, and the butler served Rufus before the family dined. A widely repeated story tells that one evening the Churchills were watching the film *Oliver Twist,* with Rufus seated on his master's lap. At the point when Bill Sikes was about to drown his dog to put the police off his track, Sir Winston put his hand over Rufus's eyes, and said, 'Don't look now … I'll tell you about it afterwards.'

The aforementioned Bill Sikes's dog was Bullseye, a bull terrier who led an appalling life, being beaten and half starved, but loyal to Sikes right to his (the dog's) ignoble end.

The great, the good and the powerful gathered for Churchill's 79th birthday party. Biographer Cita Stelzer tells that the splendid birthday cake was made to resemble a stack of all the books Churchill had written. On top was a confectionery copy of Rufus, his beloved poodle, climbing up a candle to reach a stranded cat on the top.

'Our dog chases people on a bike.
We've had to take it off him.'
*Winston Churchill*

Winston Churchill wrote a poem for his young daughter about her sick pug dog:

Pet him and kiss him and give him a hug.
Run and fetch him a suitable drug.
Wrap him up tenderly all in a rug.
That is the way to cure Puggy-Wug.

**Pug** dogs are believed to have originated in the Orient in ancient times before being introduced to Europe. They became particular favourites of Holland's royalty (the House of Orange) after a Dutch royal prince was saved from assassination by a frenzied alert given by his pet pug. In 1688, when King William and his wife Queen Mary left the Netherlands to take the English throne, they took their pet pugs with them – the first time Britain had seen the breed. Later examples arrived from China and pugs became a favourite. Some retained a royal connection, garnering the affection of Queen Victoria and later the Duke of Windsor.

'The pug is living proof that God has a sense of humour.'
*Margot Kaufman*

**Lassie** was the creation of British writer Eric Knight, who acquired a collie named Toots while he was living in California. This inspired him in 1938 to write a story published in the *Saturday Evening Post* entitled 'Lassie Come Home'. In 1943 it became a highly successful movie starring Elizabeth Taylor and Roddy McDowell. Knight never saw the film – he died in military action during World War Two before it was released.

The screen Lassie was actually male, and during the 29 years of Lassie movies, TV shows and appearances at country fairs and rodeos which followed the original hit movie, all the other Lassies were laddies.

**Rowlf**, the Muppet dog, actually began his career in 1962 in dog-food commercials. He then appeared in many television variety shows before becoming one of the first non-abstract Muppet characters in 1976. Rowlf (who was almost named Beowulf) played piano, sang, and acted as 'Dr Bob, the quack who has gone to the dogs' in over 100 Muppet shows, and continued to appear in Muppet specials and movies until 2011. He was clearly adult – or at least adolescent – in 1962, so his career spanned 49 years … very long for a dog!

**'Daddy wouldn't buy me a bow-wow'**. Composed by Joseph Tabrar in 1892, the song was launched in London by music hall star Vesta Victoria, holding a little kitten as she sang. The song was first recorded that same year, and in 1895 Toulouse-Lautrec painted May Belfort singing it. Daddy and his reluctance to buy a bow-wow surfaced frequently in shows and musicals over the decades, and was notably sung by Peter Sellars and Helen Mirren in the 1980 movie *The Fiendish Plot of Dr Fu Manchu*.

**Dog and pony show**: An elaborate presentation intended to impress and convince, either for commercial advancement or political persuasion. While not exactly suggesting fraud, the term is a somewhat disdainful put-down, since describing something as a 'dog and pony show' indicates that the speaker distrusts the validity of the message presented, regardless of its lavish presentation. The term's origin goes back a century when travelling circuses were frequent visitors to urban and rural areas. The smallest of these, lacking funds for lions, elephants and teams of acrobats, still advertised themselves as a circus – but were referred to somewhat scathingly as mere 'dog and pony shows'.

On 20 June 1837, HRH Princess Alexandrina of Kent became **HM Queen Victoria** of Great Britain and Ireland, and one year later was crowned in a sumptuous ceremony. Historian Elizabeth Longford records that immediately after the elaborate coronation ceremony in Westminster Abbey, the 18-year-old queen went straight to her apartment to wash her pet spaniel, Dash.

Queen Victoria's husband Prince Albert introduced her (and most of England) to the German breed **dachshund**. The queen took a liking to the breed (short-legged and busy, characteristics very familiar to the queen herself). A favourite dachshund in the royal circle was Dacko. When he died in 1845, the queen ordered a monument two metres high over his grave at Windsor Castle. She wrote in a letter:

> I am greatly distressed at my dear old 'Dacko' having died. The dear old dog was so attached to me and had such funny amusing ways, with large melancholy expressive eyes, and was quite part of my daily life, always in my room, and I will miss him very much.

Dachshund is a German word from *Dachs* (badger) and *Hund* (dog). They were originally bred to hunt badgers.

Queen Victoria's major celebratory occasions, such as jubilees, were marked by the granting of remission and release to various prisoners throughout the Empire, each requiring the queen's signature. But she refused to sign releases for those whose conviction had been for cruelty to animals. Historian Helen Rappaport reports that Victoria described such cruelty as 'one of the worst signs of wickedness in human nature'.

The royal love of small dogs continued. **Edward VII's** favourite dog Caesar went everywhere with him (wearing a collar which read 'I am Caesar, I belong to the King'). When the king died, Caesar took part in the State funeral procession through the streets of London, and the marble effigy of the king on his tomb includes Caesar curled up at the royal feet. Following him, George V kept Labradors, Spaniels, Sealyhams and Cairns terriers.

King George's son, the Duke of York, gave his daughter **Princess Elizabeth** a Pembroke corgi when she was very young. It was love at first sight, and corgis became part of Elizabeth's surroundings throughout her childhood, continuing into her reign as queen. The pets are fed by hand on fresh meat (lamb, rabbit or beef), with cabbage, potatoes and gravy. They famously accompany the queen around Buckingham Palace, and it has been said that the staff have advance notice of Her Majesty's movements by the scurrying noise of corgi paws which accompany her progress.

**Corgi** is derived from a combination of two Welsh words: *cor* meaning dwarf, and *ci* meaning dog. Go figure.

Not all dog stories are about courage and intelligence. Aesop's fable **'The dog and his reflection'** is a retelling of a story (and the moral that always accompanies it) dating back as far as the fifth century BC.

A dog has managed to get hold of a piece of meat and is heading across a small stream to reach a safe haven on the other side. Halfway across the stream, he looks down and sees his own reflection, enlarged by the water, thus making the piece of meat he could now see appear larger than the one he is carrying. Anxious to get hold of the larger piece, he drops his own and lunges towards the reflection, which disappears in a sudden flurry of ripples.

The dog has not only failed to gain a new piece of meat, but lost the piece he already had. The moral is: 'Who all coveteth … oft he loseth all.'

> **Give a dog a bad name**. The original full expression dates from 1760 in the form 'Give a dog a bad name and hang him', indicating that when someone has been accused of behaving badly in the past, people often expect them to behave like that in the future.

**Airedale** terriers were originally bred for chasing otters.

The American humorist, writer and cartoonist **James Thurber** loved dogs. His story 'The Dog that Bit People' (1933) was semi-biographical, semi-fictional. The star of the story was his pet Airedale terrier named Muggs, which bit people quite indiscriminately: family members, neighbours, salesmen and the occasional local dignitary. At Christmas, the family sent boxes of candy to all those people the dog had bitten during the previous year.

Thurber once said: 'Probably no man should have had so many dogs as I have had.' And of a particularly faithful pet dog, to which he would throw sticks for retrieval, he said: 'He would even have brought back a piano if you had thrown one in.'

For a long time, people in Britain were forbidden from knowing about a spaniel called Flossie. Information about her was available in Italy during 1928, but only to a limited number of people – and then to a few more in England during 1929. But to the general public, Flossie remained hidden for the next 30 years. She featured as part of a court case in 1959, then emerged in full view during 1960. From then on Flossie was able to take her place among dogs in famous works of fiction. Why the long banishment? Flossie was the canine companion of the gamekeeper Oliver Mellors, who was Lady Chatterley's lover.

D.H. Lawrence's novel **Lady Chatterley's Lover** was first published privately in Italy in 1928, then in a small private edition in Britain in 1929, but the full version of the novel only became available in 1960.

**Andy Warhol** once said, 'I never met a pet I didn't like.' His two dachshunds Amos and Archie accompanied him everywhere, and he also had a dozen cats (over a period of time), a shaggy dog called Peggy Sue and an occasional rabbit. A prized possession was a stuffed Great Dane which had died in 1930 and been placed in a see-through case. One of Warhol's most famous paintings was a portrait of a pet dachshund named Maurice, commissioned by Scottish art patron Gabrielle Keiller. The resulting 'Portrait of Maurice' was an endearing likeness of the dog, though somewhat out of the ordinary, since Maurice was shown to be blue, pink and orange.

'Dogs come when they are called. Cats take a message and get back to you.'
*Mary Bly*

'In order to keep a true perspective of one's importance, everyone should have a dog that will worship him and a cat that will ignore him.'
*Mark Twain*

'Women and cats will do as they please, and men and dogs should relax and get used to the idea.'
*Robert A. Heinlein*

**Dog watch** is a nautical term referring to evening duties of half-watches of two hours each (4pm – 6pm and 6pm – 8pm) instead of the usual four hours each. This breaks up the sequence of six watches every twenty-four hours, which would result in the same people doing the same times throughout the voyage. The origin of the name is uncertain. Some scholars accept a legend that because the two short watches were 'dodging' the symmetry of four-hour watches, the slang name 'dodge watch' came into use and was shortened to dog watch.

Other scholars prefer an explanation based on another sailor slang term, 'dog sleep', referring to the disturbed sleep experienced by those on the short shifts. And British author Patrick O'Brien came up with the tongue-in-cheek suggestion that the short watch had become known as a 'dog watch' because the usual four hours had been *cur-tailed*.

**Dogsbody** was a pejorative name seamen used in the 1800s for a mixture of dried peas which had been soaked, then boiled in a cloth. When served, it had an unfortunate appearance, leading sailors to call it, somewhat unkindly, 'dogsbody'.

As naval fare improved, the term drifted down the ranks to refer to midshipmen obliged to do work the senior officers avoided. Gradually 'dogsbody' moved from sea to shore and gained its current meaning, referring to people who are constantly at someone's beck and call, or stuck with rough or menial work – a drudge. But meanings can sometimes drift in another direction, and 'Dogsbody' has been spotted as the name of an upmarket canine grooming parlour.

Bernard of Menthon (since 1681 a Saint) built a hospice in the tenth century, which was later converted into a monastery. The Hospice of St Bernard in the Pennine Alps is first mentioned in 1125, and several centuries later became home of the famous **St Bernard dogs**. These wonderful creatures helped and rescued many travellers in distress and became the focus of legends, some of them myths, alas (they never carried little barrels of brandy). One traveller who stopped at the hospice did not need help. This was Napoleon Bonaparte, who crossed the Alps in 1800 with 40,000 troops. Captain Jean-Roche Coignet was a soldier on that crossing, and in 1851 he published his 'narrative' of that arduous journey. It contained an endearing reference to the famous hospice dogs:

> Four hundred of us grenadiers with a party of our officers entered the house of God, where men devoted to the cause of humanity are stationed to give aid and comfort to travellers. Their dogs are always on hand to guide unfortunate creatures who may have fallen in the avalanches of snow, and conduct them to this house, where every necessary comfort is provided.
>
> While our colonel and other officers were in the halls beside bright fires, we received from these venerable men a bucket of wine for every twelve men, and a quarter of a pound of Gruyere cheese and a loaf of bread for each. We were lodged in the large corridors. These good monks did everything that they possibly could, and I believe they were well treated.
>
> For our part, we pressed the good fathers' hands when we parted from them, and embraced their dogs – which caressed us as if they knew us.

The legend that St Bernard dogs carried a small barrel of brandy turned out to be a myth. Its origin is believed to have been within the imagination of English painter, Edwin Landseer. In the early 1800s, Landseer's painting 'Alpine Mastiffs Reanimating a Distressed Traveller' showed one of the St Bernard rescue dogs with a little barrel on its collar, which Landseer explained 'contained brandy'. Many people had never been to the Pennines and were inspired to believe this was the norm, so the 'brandy barrel' image became part of popular belief for generations. Shops selling 'dog accessories' quickly made St Bernard collars available (with miniature barrel attached) and the image became established, even though it was never factual.

St Bernard dogs can locate bodies buried under snow 10 ft deep (3.05 m) and can also anticipate avalanches and blizzards up to 20 minutes before they begin.

In the Welsh village of Beddgelert, a popular tourist attraction lies along a walk by the banks of the Gaslyn River. It is a broad stone plinth believed to mark the grave of a legendary thirteenth century hound owned by a medieval prince. The inscription on the monument reads:

> In the 13th century, Llewelyn, Prince of North Wales, had a palace at Beddgelert. One day he went hunting without Gelert, 'The Faithful Hound', who was unaccountably absent. On Llewelyn's return, the truant, stained and smeared with blood, joyfully sprang to meet his master. The prince, alarmed, hastened to find his son, and saw the infant's cot empty, the bedclothes and floor covered with blood. The frantic father plunged his sword into the hound's side, thinking it had killed his heir. The dog's dying yell was answered by a child's cry. Llewelyn searched and discovered his boy unharmed, but nearby lay the body of a mighty wolf which Gelert had slain. The prince, filled with remorse, is said never to have smiled again. He buried Gelert here.

Sad and colourful though the story is, pedantic historians cannot verify it – and hint that the memorial stone wasn't put in place until approximately 500 years *after* the tragic event described on it. Nevertheless, stranger stories with less 'proof' have often caught public interest and sympathy – and the tourists still go and visit it anyway.

'**Sold a pup**' means to have been deceived – and probably swindled as well. As originally used, the term is a close relative of 'a pig in a poke' – namely, a sale in the marketplace of a supposed piglet inside a bag, which, when opened at home, turns out to be something squirming but less valuable: a kitten or pup. Although this is the standard explanation for both expressions, it is hard to believe that country folk couldn't tell the difference between a mewing kitten, a yapping pup and a squealing piglet – even inside a bag!

After World War Two an appealing story emerged about an innocent-looking suburban corner store in England, selling anything and everything. However, it was also a drop-off point and contact place for a wide-ranging undercover British spy ring. The shop-owners were aware of constant German surveillance in the area looking for British undercover activity, but had to find a way to let intelligence agents know they were going into the right shop. So amid the home-made signs stuck in the window offering fresh eggs for sale and cleaning ladies for hire appeared an innocent new sign which only an Englishman would understand: **Pups sold**.

**Dogfight**. If the bone of contention escalates into a fight between two dogs, they characteristically fight in close combat. In the First World War, when air combat involved planes fighting each other at close quarters, such situations were quickly dubbed 'dogfights'. The term seemed to stick.

**Napoleon Bonaparte's** wife Josephine (whose real name wasn't Josephine, but Rose) adored her small pet pug. Legend persists that she insisted it sleep on the same bed as her, even on the night when said bed was also occupied by her new husband, Commander Napoleon Bonaparte (not yet Emperor). On that occasion, the pug objected to what Napoleon was up to, so launched himself on the naked interloper and bit him on the leg so severely that cold compresses needed to be applied for the rest of the wedding night.

The Greek philosopher **Aristotle** was surprisingly knowledgeable about the world of nature. His very comprehensive *History of Animals* (350 BC) contains a lengthy and comprehensive entry about dogs, in which he writes:

> The male as a rule lifts his leg to void urine when six months old; some at a later period, when eight months old, some before they reach six months. In a general way one may put it that they do so when they are out of puppyhood. The bitch squats down when she voids urine; it is a rare exception that she lifts the leg to do so. The bitch bears twelve pups at the most, but usually five or six; occasionally a bitch will bear one only. The two sexes have intercourse with each other at all periods of life.

Dogs figure twice in stories surrounding the 1922 discovery by Howard Carter and Lord Carnarvon of treasures from *c*.1397 BC in the tomb of **Tutankhamun**. Amongst them was a large square plinth of gilded wood, on which lay a life-sized dog statue in a crouching position, with pricked-up ears and an air of great alertness. Wrapped around the statue was a shawl of fine linen. The dog's paws were guarding an ivory painter's palette inscribed with the name Princess Merytaten.

Then there was the famous 'curse' associated with the opening of the tomb – now regarded as possibly spurious. It may have been invented by a journalist, frustrated that he was denied entry, then taken up by the excavators, who wanted to discourage people from visiting the site so that they could continue their work unimpeded. One persistent part of the legend is that when Lord Carnarvon died (in Egypt), his dog Suzie (in England) gave a mournful howl and dropped dead at exactly the same time. Evidence for the story is frail, however, the main sticking point being the blithe disregard for time zones. Lord Carnarvon died at 2am Egyptian time, which would have been midnight in England. But the exact time of Suzie's death varied considerably in each re-telling, and whether or not there was a witness remained uncertain. But the legend lives on.

# Sled dogs

In New York's Central Park there stands an impressive statue of an equally impressive dog: Balto, a Siberian husky. The statue commemorates an extraordinary event in Alaska in 1925, when there was a breakout of diphtheria in the city of Nome, which is close to the Arctic Circle and isolated behind several mountain ranges. It was winter, daylight hours were limited and sea access frozen. Winter supplies were customarily brought by dog sled, but Nome urgently needed diphtheria antitoxin, so something remarkable was called for. A total of 150 sled dogs in relays covered the 670 miles (1074 kms) in whiteout blizzard conditions across Alaska and the iced Bering Sea in five-and-a-half days, bringing the serum to Nome and saving it from an incipient epidemic. The lead sled dog on the final stretch into the city was Balto, who became very famous – a dog celebrity. The statue of Balto was unveiled in Central Park later that year and became a popular tourist attraction. It is intended as a tribute to all the huskies involved. The inscription reads:

Dedicated to the indomitable spirit of the sled dogs that relayed antitoxin 600 miles over rough ice, treacherous waters, through arctic blizzards to the relief of stricken Nome in the winter of 1925.

Endurance, Fidelity, Intelligence.

Shortly after the dramatic serum trek to Nome, Balto himself was taken to Hollywood to appear in a filmed version of the event: *Balto's Race to Nome* (1925). Seventy years later a full-length animation movie *Balto* was released (1995) telling a somewhat fanciful version of the trek, followed by another equally fanciful animation, *Balto's Wolf Quest*, in 2002.

**Mush** is a word associated with teams of sled dogs, and other activities and sports which include dogs and speed. 'Mush' is an instruction to maintain or increase speed – i.e. 'Hurry up, keep going.' It is believed to be a modified form of the French *marchons*, which translates as the colloquial 'Let's get going'. It is sometimes called 'mushing', while the sled-driver can be called a 'musher'.

**Dogfish** is a name applied to various kinds of shark. The likeness to dogs implied in the name is believed to be because dogfish hunt the sea in packs.

The Earl of Home was accustomed in 1730 to fish for salmon from the River Tweed. In *The Domesday Book of Giant Salmon*, British fishing expert Fred Buller recounts that Lord Home's pet **Newfoundland dog** was even better at catching salmon then the earl himself: the dog was credited with catching up to 20 in a morning.

A neighbouring landowner, Lord Tankerville, took up arms against this unfair way of reducing the local supply of salmon. Buller writes:

> The then Lord Tankerville instituted a process against the dog. The case was brought before the Court of Session, and the process was entitled The Earl of Tankerville versus a Dog, the property of the Earl of Home.

> Judgment was given in favour of the dog.

In *The Independent* Keith Elliot commented: 'I'll bet that dog never exaggerated the size of his catch.'

**Richard Wagner** was devoted to his King Charles spaniel named Peps, who actually participated in his master's composing. Wagner's biographer H.T. Finck records that Peps constantly sat near Wagner when the composer was at the piano. Sometimes Peps would leap onto the table and peer into Wagner's face, howling piteously. Wagner would ask: 'What? It does not suit you?' then shake the dog's paw and say, 'I will do thy bidding gently.' Constantly following this procedure, Wagner claimed that Peps had helped him compose *Tannhäuser*.

Unkind commentators later opined that Peps was the only critic Wagner ever listened to.

**Haydn**, **Beethoven** and **Chopin** all wrote music about poodles. Haydn's song 'The clever and zealous poodle' tells of an ingenious dog which found his master's lost coin. Beethoven's song 'Elegy on the death of a poodle' reflects the sadness of anyone who has lost a beloved dog. But Chopin's jaunty 'Valse du petit chien' (commonly called the 'Minute Waltz') is a keyboard image reflecting the friskiness of his mistress Georges Sand's poodle puppies.

'**Walking the dog**'. In Britain, the city of Newcastle is home to Newcastle Brown Ale which has been brewed there for many decades. The dark brown ale has a notably rich and hearty flavour, described also as a bit tangy and with a nutty aroma. In its home territory, the ale is often referred to as 'the dog', based on a local legend that men wanting to slip down to the pub for some Newcastle Brown would tell their wives they were 'walking the dog'. The popularity of Newcastle Brown Ale has spread well beyond Newcastle, and aficionados as far away as the United States cheerfully repeat the 'walking the dog' phrase, even when there is no need to. Venues in California sometimes host a 'walking the dog day' where Newcastle Brown Ale is served to enthusiastic patrons of similar tastes in ale, who join in *bonhomie* to drink Newcastle Brown – 'the dog'.

'**Dog's nose**' is the name of a rather esoteric cocktail, a strange-sounding mixture which has a reputation of taking the chill off a cold day. Charles Dickens knew about it: 'dog's nose' is described in *Pickwick Papers* as made of warm porter, moist sugar and gin, with a fresh grating of nutmeg to adorn the foam (porter was a dark, sweet ale). A modern version keeps the basic gin but adds a splash of cointreau and a twist of orange, topped up with dry stout. The reason for the name 'dog's nose' is presumed to be that a dog's nose is wet and black. Go figure.

**Sigmund Freud** believed that keeping his friendly pet Chow dog Jogi in his consulting room during psychotherapy sessions was a comfort to patients. Psychology professor Stanley Coren, in his book *What Do Dogs Know?*, reports that in addition to the calming effect of the dog's presence, her behaviour assisted Freud in assessing a patient's problems. Jogi would sit close to a patient she felt to be calm and allow herself to be patted, but if she sensed any tension she would move well away. If she suspected that the patient was telling untruths, Jofi would scratch to be let out the door. If she came back, Freud would say, 'Jofi has decided to give you another chance.'

Freud hated birthdays but loved his pet dogs. So his family would arrange a birthday party for him with only his three dogs present. They would wear party hats and be seated round a table while Freud served them cake. Tucked in the collar of each animal was a poem 'written' by the dog, which the master of psychoanalysis took delight in reading to the dog who 'wrote' it.

**Doggerel** is bad poetry with faulty rhymes, strained rhythm, unclear imagery and little literary value. It has been called doggerel since at least 1387, when a character in Chaucer's 'Tale of Sir Thopas' declares that the tale told by Sir Thopas 'may well be rhyme doggerel'. Any connection with actual dogs is unclear, though it has been suggested that inelegant poetry was being compared to puppy clumsiness or perhaps with food which only dogs would find attractive.

According to the British North America Philatelic Society, the world's first **postage stamp** featuring a dog was printed in 1887 and released in 1888 by Newfoundland (before it entered into confederation with Canada). The stamp was printed in three colours – black, red and orange – and the dog pictured was, of course, a Newfoundland.

The **flag** of the federal territory of Yukon in Canada has its own heraldic coat of arms showing:

> Stylised mountains inset with gold coins (acknowledging the mineral resources and the Klondike), vertical parallel wavy lines representing the area's rivers, a circle filled with a pattern representing the territory's abundant fur-bearing animals, surrounded by a red cross acknowledging England.

And atop it all, standing proudly on a mound of snow, is a fine figure of an Alaskan Malamute dog.

The **Alaskan Malamute** dog dates back several thousand years, and the breed played a significant part in helping to maintain the early dwellers above the Arctic Circle. They continue to pull heavy loads of freight supplies to camps and villages there, and were closely involved with the miners in the 1896 Klondike gold rush. They also aided Rear Admiral Richard Byrd in his South Pole expeditions, and served in World War Two as search and rescue dogs.

'**How much is that doggie in the window?**', first released in 1952, became one of the most popular of all dog songs. Hit recordings by Patti Page (USA) and Lita Roza (Britain) were followed by a large number of other versions: comedy animations by Wallace and Gromit; television shows such as *Eastenders* and *Seinfeld*; *Discworld* (sung in Latation!); *Peanuts* (Snoopy loves the song) and Homer and Jethro. British Prime Minister Margaret Thatcher chose Lita Roza's recording as her favourite of all time.

**More dog songs**: 'Me and you and a dog named Boo'; 'Puppy love'; 'Bird dog'; 'Old Blue'; 'Hot dog'; 'Gonna buy me a dog'; 'Dirty old egg-suckin' dog'; 'Snoopy and the Red Baron'; 'I love my dog'; and 'Seamus' (on the Pink Floyd recording, Seamus the dog sings along).

**Snoopy** the cartoon beagle was born at the Daisy Hill Puppy Farm, and first appeared in the *Peanuts* cartoon strip in October 1950. He continued appearing for 50 years, but never aged a day. Snoopy's attempts to write a novel all began with 'It was a dark and stormy night …' – a genuine line borrowed from Edward Bulwer-Lytton's 1830 novel, *Paul Clifford*.

# Record makers

An Australian cattle dog in the state of Victoria died in November 1939. This would not have been so remarkable – except that Bluey had been born on 7 June 1910. After his death *The Guinness Book of Records* acknowledged that Bluey's lifespan of 29 years and 160 days gave him the longest recorded lifespan of any known dog.

Other Guinness records include:

* The loudest measured bark by a dog was 108 dB, produced by white German shepherd Daz in Finsbury Park, London, on 15 June 2009. (100 decibels is equivalent to a chain saw, pneumatic drill, farm tractor.)

* In 1978 an eight-year-old St Bernard belonging to Thomas and Ann Irwin in Michigan weighed 305 lbs (138.34 kgs).

* A Great Dane in Milton Keynes, Buckinghamshire, England, reached a height of 42 inches (106 cms).

* A greyhound on a track can reach a speed of 41.7 mph (66.7 km/h). A Saluki runs at very slightly behind the greyhound's speed – but has more stamina and can sustain its speed for longer.

* Dogs in industrial or security employment can learn to be effective 'climbers'. An Alsatian with De Beers mining company in Pretoria could leap and scramble over a wall 11 ft 3ins high (3.43 m).

* In 2004 a Neopolitan Bull Mastiff called Tia, in Cambridgeshire, England, became pregnant and grew so large that movement was difficult and a scan showed 'about ten' puppies. A caesarean was arranged for her, and Tia produced 24 puppies – a world record at the time.

* Between 1961 and 1969 a male greyhound named Timmy of Regent's Park, London, fathered 2404 registered puppies – and at least 600 others which weren't registered.

* In 1925 a Doberman Pinscher police dog in South Africa successfully tracked a wanted thief 100 miles (160 km) across the vast Great Karoo desert by scent alone.

* Trep, a drug-sniffing dog in Florida, was taken to a police training academy to demonstrate dog-sniffing skills and management. To test him, police cadets were given ten small packets of marijuana to hide around the building. Great was the cadets' embarrassment when Trep effortlessly found eleven.

Trep also once had a search warrant issued in his name by a magistrate who wanted to ensure that the dog would be admitted with the Dade County police to search a house suspected of a drugs connection.

'To rub someone's nose in it' is to let someone know they have committed a mistake or blunder and then to remind them of it in such a way that they never forget it. The phrase has its origin in a practice which some people think is an effective way of house-training a puppy when he urinates inside the house: rub his nose in it.

'You can't teach an old dog new tricks' is a very familiar and self-explanatory saying. It first surfaced in 1523, but was more simply worded in John Ray's *Proverbs* (1670): 'An old dog will learn no tricks.'

'Have a bone to pick' is to have a point to argue or a complaint to settle. A dog will cheerfully enjoy 'picking' and chomping at a bone to extract the last possible morsel of nourishment from it – usually alone. But there are often fireworks if another dog shows interest in the bone. It is to this tension that the saying refers: that an unwelcome discussion is about to take place concerning a matter about which one participant feels heated while the other is prepared to defend his position. Since the 1500s, a matter of dispute has been described as 'a bone of contention'.

'**Doggone**' is an exclamation of annoyance, exasperation and disappointment. The term has been in use since the mid-1800s and is generally believed to be a euphemistic contraction of *God damn*, possibly through a Scottish contraction of the same term 'dagone'. It is often said as 'doggone it'.

**Dog's bollocks**: the top, the best, the most admirable. 'Bollocks' came into use in the 1700s as a slang term for testicles. As a stand-alone word it is used as a put-down: 'bollocks' means rubbish, 'bollocking' means a severe chastising and 'dropping a bollock' means a big mistake. How this usage reversed into a term of high praise when referring to the testicles of a dog has never been clear. One possibility put forward is that because a dog's bollocks are often quite prominent, there could be a connection between the word 'bollocks' and the word 'outstanding'!

The much-honoured Japanese writer **Junichiro Tanizaki** published his *Childhood Memoir* in 1957. When still a child, his junior school was near a carved stone shrine – that of Lord Sugawara no Michizane, who had been deified as Tenjin-sama. The children were diligently taught the complex tiny brush-strokes of Japanese writing, and Tanizaki recalls:

> When a writing brush wore out, we would take it to Tenjin-sama's shrine and place it between the legs of the Korean lion dogs that guard the deity. There was always quite a bundle of these used children's brushes.

Why? Because the god and his dogs were reputed to confer on children the gift of good writing.

**Akita Inu**. This Japanese breed originated in the Akita prefecture in the northern island of Honshu. *Inu* is sometimes included in the name, being a Japanese word for 'dog'.

**Hachiko** was a Japanese Akita dog which walked
to the local train station every day to meet his master,
Professor Ueno, when he returned from work at the University
of Tokyo. One day in 1925 the professor had a fatal stroke
while at work and did not come home. Hachiko had to be
housed with a different family, but for nine years he walked to
the Shibuya station every day at the appropriate time, waiting
for his master – who never came.

Hachiko became infirm and died in 1935. But by then his
fame had spread and he was seen as a symbol of devotion and
family loyalty. A bronze statue of Hachiko was erected at the
Shibuya station and still stands there.

# Alexander Graham Bell

Alexander Graham Bell's father and grandfather were both elocution teachers. Grandfather's work influenced George Bernard Shaw when he wrote *Pygmalion* (which later became *My Fair Lady*). In the original play, one of his books is mentioned by Professor Henry Higgins ('I'll take her down first in Bell's *Visible Speech*'), and one of Shaw's dedications of *Pygmalion* is to Alexander Melville Bell.

Young Alexander found he could effectively communicate with his increasingly deaf mother by careful lip movements, which led him to take an interest in teaching language to the deaf. His interest in sound reproduction caused him to consider associating speech sounds with the recognition of mouth movements. He spent a considerable time experimenting with a subject which couldn't say words at all – his dog. After encouraging the dog to produce long and amiable growls, he would move the Skye terrier's jaw up and down to change the emitted sound, then alter the sound again by pushing a finger up and down under the muzzle. The terrier, co-operative to a fault, allowed all this and eventually succeeded in making a noise – without knowing why – which sounded roughly like 'ah-ma' (for which read 'grandma', without consonants).

Further manipulation of the jaw-plus-growl produced a dog version of 'oo' and 'ow'. Nobody is pretending that the dog learned to speak, but Alexander's fingers, playing his jaw like a piano, managed to produce from the dog a sequence of sounds which even without consonants could roughly be interpreted as 'How are you, Grandma?' Mission accomplished. Alexander Graham Bell had satisfied himself that a deaf person, when shown differing mouth shapes, could gradually (though perhaps more quickly than a dog) learn to emit sounds which matched the words they wanted to say. Bell became a teacher of deaf mute children. In his spare time he modified and patented the invention of the telephone.

# Greyfriars Bobby

Legend has it that Bobby, a Skye terrier, was the inseparable companion of an Edinburgh night-watchman, John Gray, who died in 1858. Gray was buried in Greyfriars Kirkyard, Edinburgh. For the next 14 years, Bobby wandered the graveyard every day and sat on the grave waiting for his master, who never returned. A nearby restaurant honoured the dog's vigil and provided food. Bobby's devotion became famous, and since he had no known owner or licence, Sir William Chambers, Lord Provost of Edinburgh himself paid for a licence, so Bobby was effectively 'owned' by the City Council. Sir William also had a special collar made, inscribed: 'Greyfriars Bobby from the Lord Provost, 1867, licensed'. It is now in the Edinburgh Museum.

Bobby died in 1872, and while he could not be buried in consecrated ground, he was interred just inside the gate. A year later, Baroness Burdett-Coutts arranged for a granite stand with a statue of Bobby on top to be installed there. The inscription reads:

Greyfriars Bobby. Died 14 January 1872
aged 16 years.

Let his loyalty and devotion be a lesson to us all.

Bobby's story has been told many times – in books, television, songs and several movies. Since the mid-1860s, when his story came to public attention, many tourists have visited the site and later the statue, and there have even been guided tours.

But is the legend completely true? Over a hundred years after Bobby's death and with the legend well established, Dr Jan Bondeson, a senior lecturer at Cardiff University, had some doubts and applied diligent research to elements of the story which could still be tracked down. Alas, his conclusion was firm: Greyfriars Bobby was partly a hoax and an illusion! There is no actual evidence for the identity of Bobby's 'master', nor is there any certainty that the dog frequenting the churchyard had ever been attached to anyone buried there.

Dr Bondeson also studied available likenesses of Bobby during his 14 years' graveside devotion, and came to the conclusion that two different dogs were involved. By appearance, age and breed, he ascertained that the original Bobby had probably died in 1867. But by then the legend was established, and it was 'good for local business' that tourists kept coming and attended the 'restaurant which gave Bobby food'. So a replacement was hastily found (according to Dr Bondeson, illustrations then show a younger dog of a different breed) and taught the graveyard routine. But researched proof or not, Dr Bondeson acknowledges that the public probably prefers a legend to the truth. He told the *Daily Mail*: 'It won't ever be possible to debunk the story of Greyfriars Bobby – he's a living legend, the most faithful dog in the world, and bigger than all of us.'

Cynossema is a promontory on the south-eastern coast of Turkey. The historian **Plutarch** recounts a story about a wealthy Greek politician called Xanthippus, who in 479 BC owned a very faithful dog. When invasion by the Persians threatened Athens, many citizens fled the city in crowded boats. Xanthippus commanded the last boat to leave, and since it was seriously overladen, there was no room for his dog, which he hoped would escape to the hills and survive. But the dog jumped into the sea and refused to leave his master, faithfully swimming alongside the galley for 16 kilometres to the island of Salamis, where the poor animal collapsed from exhaustion and died. Griefstricken, Xanthippus buried his dog and named the place Cynossema, meaning 'the tomb of the dog'. The name remains to this day.

**Feisty** is a word with a bizarre history. It is a descendant of the word 'fist', which once had two meanings. As everyone knows, a fist is a clenched hand. But during the 1400s 'fist' developed a

secondary meaning, politely described as 'a small backward escape of wind, accompanied by an unpleasant smell'. Since this phenomenon was (possibly quite unfairly) associated with dogs, the expression 'fysting cur' came into use in America c. 1800. The 'fysting' narrowed down through usage and became 'feist', applied (again possibly unfairly) to highly active dogs. Eventually the word became 'feisty', meaning exuberant, spirited, mildly aggressive – and the association with dogs and smell was forgotten.

**Cynic**. The ancient Greek word for dog – *kuon* – was modified in Latin as *canis*, which in English became 'canine'. Although the Greeks were widely acknowledged as dog lovers, the same word which gave us 'canine' also developed into the word 'cynic'. The link was that members of a restive and critical philosophical group in ancient times were known as 'the snarlers' – and a version of the word for 'dog' was used to describe them. This developed a parallel meaning of its own: a cynic (someone morose and hard to please) as opposed to a dog (the epitome of friendliness).

Eighteen dogs helped Norwegian explorer **Roald Amundsen** become the first person to reach the South Pole, a feat they accomplished on 3 December 1911. The assistance of the Greenland sledge dogs has been seen as a vital advantage in aiding the Norwegian party to reach the Pole, which rival British explorer Robert Falcon Scott failed to do. For transport in the icy conditions Scott had relied instead on horses.

A Jack Russell terrier called Bothie accompanied **Sir Ranulph Fiennes** on his Transglobe expedition (1979–82) and so became the first dog to set paws on *both* the North and South Poles. During his six weeks at the South Pole, Bothie took part in the first cricket match played at the Pole, and his enthusiastic fielding on a somewhat unorthodox surface was a factor in Sir Ranulph's team beating the American scientists' team.

# *Howl*

*Howl* was a genuine musical composition for concert performance, featuring a human choir and several solo dogs. Its premiere in 1980, in Carnegie Hall no less, was led by the highly respected musician and composer Kirk Nurock. Nurock's pedigree was impressive. A graduate of the Juilliard School, he had worked with Leonard Bernstein, Bette Midler, Dizzy Gillespie and many others, but he also loved dogs. *Howl* did not require the dogs to have musical qualifications, or even to start and stop 'singing' according to the conductor's signal. But Nurock had auditioned 32 dogs to find three which would just burst into song without restraint when they heard a piano play and other people singing.

And this is exactly what they did – with generous descants of howls, barks and growls throughout the three sections of the 24-minute suite. The performance was a huge success. To enthusiastic applause, the human chorus bowed, and the dog soloists barked their thanks. The *New York Times* reported:

> The highlight of the evening was the world premiere of Mr Nurock's *Howl*. A human chorus, alternately barking or cooing sweetly, was joined by five of 'man's best friends' who provided their own bestial improvisations. 'We too are animals,' explains Mr Nurock's notes, but despite some disturbingly amusing howling, the canine soloists – Bonnie, Wilhelmena, Bogus, Gideon and Isadora Duncan – seemed far more natural.

Following the success of *Howl*, Kirk Nurock composed a Sonata for piano and dogs, which debuted in 1983. This too was an audience-pleaser – so much so that Nurock was invited to perform it on the David Letterman television show, with two of the dogs which had featured in his concert performances. Unabashed by lights and microphones, the concert canines howled up a television storm, interspersed with staccato yaps and contralto rumblings. The audience loved it (and many felt that Mozart would have loved it too).

American musician **Laurie Anderson** and her rock legend husband Lou Reed once held a concert performance contrived solely for dogs. It was staged on the forecourt of the Sydney Opera House. A four-piece band, including violin, synthesisers, high-pitched slide whistles and whale calls, presented a surreal programme featuring 'white noise' music (with no tune, but 'soothing' qualities), plus rhythm and beat items. As planned, some of the pieces were beyond the range of human ears, but a joyous audience of 1000 dogs reacted with excited frenzies of barks and howls which almost drowned out the performers. Laurie Anderson described them as 'a wonderful audience – the dogs were really grooving and enjoying themselves. Very well behaved too – no dog fights!'

Although the venue was part of the world-famous Sydney Opera House, there was no place in the programme for *The Barker of Seville* or *The Marriage of Fido*.

The international singing-and-comedy duo **Flight of the Conchords** were unaware that epilepsy could affect dogs. But having heard of someone whose dog was epileptic, they penned a song ('We're both in love with a sexy lady') which included a plea about 'puppies not born so lucky'. Their song encourages people to give 'a donation, to save a shaking dalmatian', provide support to 'make a setter feel better', help a golden retriever 'having a seizure', or a 'labrador shaking on the floor'.

Though
they
might
enjoy a snack of
**chocolate** – indeed
even seek one – it is very
dangerous for dogs. Chocolate
contains a chemical called theobromine
which can cause vomiting, diarrhoea, seizures,
hyperactivity and heart problems in dogs – and
sometimes even death. Neither does their system welcome
more than a minimum amount of salt – so bacon, pork and
soy products should only be offered in moderation (post-
Christmas ham-bone scraps, although relished at the time, can
result in a visit to a vet's surgery). An overdose of tomatoes
and onions can cause problems too, though small amounts
(say in a Bolognese leftover) won't cause trouble.

Other foods which are dangerous to dogs are avocados,
raisins, caffeine and sugar, though not in small amounts. One
of the worst things for dogs is ex-radiator water, either lying
unnoticed in a puddle after being drawn out (to be replaced),
or left in a vessel which the dog can reach into. There are
dog-dangerous plants too: oleander is bad, and many canines
are allergic to common ivy and need to be discouraged from
plunging through it. Cornell University's Department of Animal
Science also warns that dogs should not munch on lily-of-the
valley, jasmine, hyacinths, wisteria, rhubarb leaves, lantana,
foxgloves, buttercups, daphne and daffodils.

**Mutt**. The word's history involves two species: one with four legs and one with two. Derived from the old French *moutoun* (sheep), in English 'mutton' became associated with cooked sheep flesh rather than with the animal itself. But the perception of sheep as stupid gave rise to 'muttonhead' (1803), meaning blockhead or dullard. Over the course of the following century, 'muttonhead' gradually moved away from being an insult or put-down between people. Abbreviated to 'mutt', it became a general reference to dogs, especially those of doubtful parentage. By then 'muttonhead', indicating someone who is ignorant, had been replaced by 'meathead'.

In Dr Seuss's book *The Grinch Who Stole Christmas*, the grouch doctor has a faithful dog Max, of uncertain ancestry. He refers to Max simply as 'mutt'.

Comic characters called Mutt and Jeff appeared in 1907. In rhyming slang, 'mutton' or 'mutt 'n' jeff' means deaf.

> To coin a phrase …
> We know what a misogynist is, but what about a **misdogynist**?
> If your dog is too cute for words, perhaps you need a **phodographer**.

**Dogged:** obstinate, tenacious, determined. Dating from *c*.1325, the word is believed to refer to an image of a dog clamping jaws on something it intends to keep and remaining clamped thereon.

When pioneer Scottish settlers in the nineteenth century arrived in the southern part of New Zealand, the terrain was a challenge – but they had brought their dogs. In the area known as the Mackenzie country (where part of *The Lord of the Rings* would be filmed over a hundred years later) the mountainous plateau might have remained unfarmed had it not been for the hard work of the shepherds and their tireless dogs. In 1968 a beautiful bronze statue of a magnificent collie sheep dog was placed on a huge rock on the shores of Lake Tekapo and ceremoniously unveiled by the then Governor-General, Sir Arthur Porritt. The inscription on the plaque reads:

> This monument was erected by the runholders of the Mackenzie County and those who also appreciate the value of the collie dog, without the help of which the grazing of the mountain country would be impossible.

# Top dog or underdog

Dogs in any grouping – a wild pack or even just a domestic group – have an 'alpha' who is dominant. The term shifted to the popular sport of dog-fighting – with two references, one actual and one predicted. During a fight the superior dog could be seen on top. If a particular dog had a track record for often achieving this supremacy, those taking bets on a forthcoming fight would refer to that participant as a 'top dog' while a newcomer, or fighter with an unimpressive track record, would be the 'under dog'. Both terms moved away from dog-fighting and into wide metaphorical use following the publication in 1859 of a poem by the American poet David Barker:

### The Under Dog in the Fight

I know that the world, the great big world,
From the peasant up to the king,
Has a different tale from the tale I tell,
And a different song to sing.
But for me, and I care not a single fig
If they say I am wrong or right,
I shall always go for the weaker dog,
For the under dog in the fight.

I know that the world, that the great big world,
Will never a moment stop –
To see which dog may be in the fault,
But will shout for the dog on top.
But for me I shall never pause to ask
Which dog may be in the right.
For my heart will beat, while it beats at all,
For the under dog in the fight.

There is a theory that the terms 'top dog' and 'underdog'
originated from their use by sawyers in saw pits – that
with the two-handed saws used on tree trunks set
horizontally above a pit, the senior sawyer on the upper
surface of the trunk was the 'top dog' and the man
beneath was the 'under dog'. Alas, there is no certain
evidence for the theory. Dog-fights seem to be the answer.

# Rural dogs

In New Zealand, the resort of Queenstown presents two wildly popular events in mid-winter (June/July) honouring the largely rural dogs of the Otago province. For one afternoon, the international ski resort of Coronet Peak is host to the local canines in the snow-based Dog Derby. Several dozen dogs travel with their owners for an unaccustomed ride up the mountain in a ski lift. Then at the 'Start' command, all the masters, with their dogs close by, rush down the piste as fast as possible – on foot, no skis, frequently sliding on their backsides, then stumbling back up on their feet, all the while with their faithful hounds excitedly keeping pace. The dogs cope magnificently with the craziness of the event and boldly tackle the occasional obstacle course set up to make things even trickier. There is often mayhem, always a lot of noise (described by the organisers as 'barking, shouting, and rustic language'), adding up to huge enjoyment. The trip down can take about 30 minutes. The fastest dog and master to arrive at the mountain base are declared the winners, with major credit going to the dog.

Later the same day, in the central town square, comes the Dog Barking contest. Shepherds and farmers come into town with their faithful four-legged best friends to take part in a hilarious public contest to find the loudest barker. Each dog and master together must step onto a small stage, where hay bales have been pushed together to make a podium, on which the dog is encouraged to perform, giving its best bark. The participating dogs are often

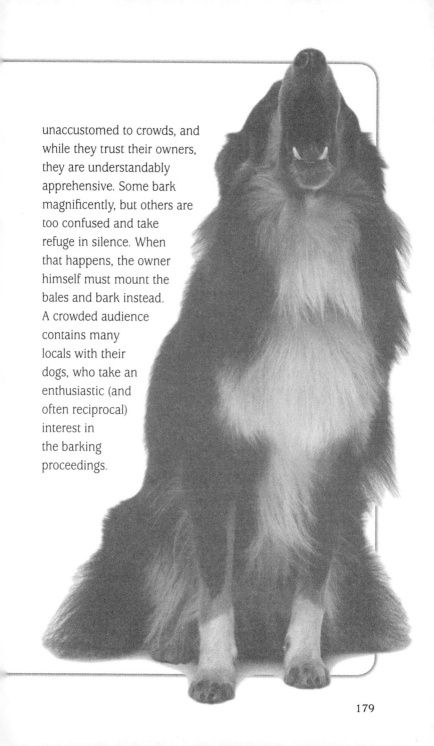

unaccustomed to crowds, and while they trust their owners, they are understandably apprehensive. Some bark magnificently, but others are too confused and take refuge in silence. When that happens, the owner himself must mount the bales and bark instead. A crowded audience contains many locals with their dogs, who take an enthusiastic (and often reciprocal) interest in the barking proceedings.

A **'designer dog'** is the term used to describe a deliberate cross-breeding of two different types, in the hope that the best features of each will be retained in the new mix. Sometimes the combination is deliberately reflected in the name of the new breed. For example, the versatile (and apparently partner-amiable) poodle has been part of several new breeds: Cockapoo, Yorkipoo, Pekepoo, Shih-poo, Maltipoo, Labradoodle and Schnoodle (a poodle and a Schnauzer). There's also a Puggle (pug and beagle), a Boxweiler (Boxer and Rottweiler), a Bassador (Basset hound and Labrador) and an Afador (Afghan hound and Labrador).

The phenomenon can happen accidentally, as with a Dachshund belonging to Britain's Princess Margaret, which became matey (literally) with Queen Elizabeth's Pembroke corgi. Result: a dorgi.

Professor Stanley Coren reports: 'A man once told me that his dog was half pit bull and half poodle. He claimed that it wasn't much good as a guard dog, but it was a vicious gossip.'

In 1977 the long-running British television science-fiction series *Dr Who* introduced a **robot dog** character called K9. He had wide general knowledge, extraordinary computer intelligence and a scary laser inside his metallic nose. K9 proved to be an intriguing part of Dr Who's cosmic world, and continued to appear in various episodes and spin-offs for over 30 years.

The Kennel Club of England, known to take **dog breeding** very seriously, commissioned a portrait of Queen Elizabeth II in 1975. Her Majesty consented, and it was agreed that she would be depicted with one of her favourite dogs … which turned out to be the aforementioned dorgi. Club officials were somewhat taken aback, since 'crossbreed' is not a welcome word among serious breeders. But the queen proceeded with her chosen pose, and the portrait was hung in the Kennel Club headquarters, thus bringing what is said to be the only crossbreed ever allowed into those almost-sacred premises.

Legend has it that when the portrait arrived at the club, a member was heard to exclaim: 'Dachshunds were evolved to chase badgers down holes and corgis to round up cattle. So if anyone loses a herd of cattle down a badger hole – dorgis are just the dogs to get them out.'

**The quick brown fox jumps over the lazy dog**. The word 'panagram' is derived from the Greek *pan*, meaning all, and *gramma,* meaning letters. Thus: 'all letters'. The name is given to test sentences which include all 26 letters of the English alphabet, the most famous of which tells us about a fox jumping over a dog. This fanciful happening is mentioned as early as 1885 in an American teaching manual as a suggestion for typewriting keyboard practice. Although there are other panagrams, the 'fox and dog' rapidly became a favourite among English-speaking typewriting teachers – and later computer trainees.

By the way, the sentence must be in the present tense, because 'jumps' is the only word in which the letter 's' occurs. Write 'jumped' and you have just 25 letters.

> **Afghan hounds** are believed by hunters in Afghanistan to have been the only dog representatives on Noah's ark.

**Shaggy dog story**. This expression, which has been in use since the 1930s, refers to a complicated and apparently endless tale. Its exact origin is unclear, though it is possible to discern a connection between a wildly unfocused story and an unkempt dog with a dishevelled coat.

**Sir Paul McCartney's** Old English sheepdog called Martha provided the name of his song 'Martha, My Dear', though it's believed that the lyrics describe McCartney's early fiancée, Jane Asher.

**Johnny Cash** had two dogs called Hell and Redemption.

The only image on the cover of **Eric Clapton's** album *There's One in Every Crowd* is the singer's dog Jeep – in very lugubrious mood, and resting on what might well be a coffin. But in happier vein, Jeep is also referred to in George Harrison's song, 'I Remember Jeep'.

**Elton John's** cocker spaniel Arthur was best man at Elton's civil partnership ceremony with David Furnish.

**Marilyn Monroe** and **Arthur Miller** owned a Basset hound named Hugo, of which Marilyn was particularly fond. Writer Norman Rosten and photographer Sam Shaw recounted in their book *Marilyn Among Friends* that because a Basset is so low slung, Marilyn told them she was anxious when the dog hurried over rocky ground, in case his penis struck a stone. She would call out and warn him: 'Be careful, Hugo!'

**Elvis Presley** had several pet dogs, many with memorable names: Baba, Edmund, Getlo, Muffin, Stuff and Sweet Pea. But as far as anyone knows, he never owned a hound dog.

# Mathematics

When Timothy J. Pennings of Michigan threw a tennis ball into a lake for his dog Elvis to fetch, he noticed that the pooch didn't necessarily run straight from where he was standing, but sometimes galloped a short distance away at a tangent before rushing from that point into the water. A mathematics professor, Pennings undertook a series of trials, throwing balls at various angles into the lake for Elvis to plunge in and retrieve. Pennings marked the throwing-point, then ran and marked the point at the lake's edge to which the dog had run before plunging into the water. He then constructed algebraic equations in which '$r$' signified running speed, '$s$' was the swimming speed, '$A$' was the throwing point, and '$C$-$D$' the distance between jumping in and bringing the ball back to '$A$'.

He came to the surprising conclusion that although a dog might be puzzled if it were shown an algebraic equation, Elvis instinctively understood the principle perfectly. By a super-rapid calculation within the canine brain, he could calculate the launch-point which would be the shortest distance to forge through water towards the desired quarry. Since a dog can run faster than he can swim, by running to the launch-spot of the shortest swimming distance he was able to deliver the ball back in the shortest time.

After many more similar practical exercises, and examining them as strict scientific equations, Professor Pennings cheerfully acknowledged that while dogs do not know calculus and never do equations, they are nevertheless equipped with an amazing inbuilt calculating system of their own, which in the space of a second can put into action 'the uncanny way in which nature often finds optimal solutions' (and more rapidly than anyone using a protractor and a set square).

In **Salem**, **Massachusetts**, the infamous witch trials in 1692 sent several people to their death, condemned in a context of community hysteria of being in magical league with the Devil. One rather complex way of judging whether women were witches was to secretly obtain some of their urine, bake it in a cake and give it to a dog. If the dog behaved in a weird, undoglike way, then clearly it was bewitched – and therefore the donor of the urine must be similarly afflicted! As a result of this delusional hysteria, two dogs were hanged because of their believed 'affiliation with witchcraft'.

One of the unexpected creatures **Alice** met when she was in Wonderland was an enormous puppy, whose sheer size made Alice nervous that he might be considering eating her. She threw a twig, which he loped away to retrieve while Alice hid behind a huge thistle. She then ran and climbed a giant-sized mushroom … where she found a blue caterpillar smoking a pipe.

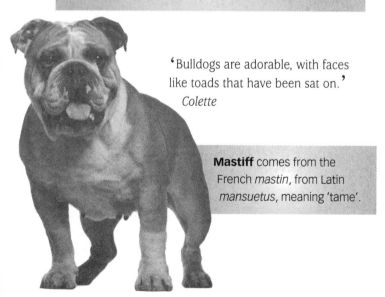

'Bulldogs are adorable, with faces like toads that have been sat on.'
*Colette*

**Mastiff** comes from the French *mastin*, from Latin *mansuetus*, meaning 'tame'.

**The dog rose** (*Rosa canina*) has a familiar, simply shaped, single flower. It has been said that the appellation 'dog' signified that the rose had no perfume and thus lacked worth. Kinder scholars say that its 'dog' name comes from the ancient belief that an infusion of its roots was prized as a treatment for the bite from a rabid dog. Whatever the origin of its name, the dog rose's attractive bloom was frequently used in medieval symbolism of aristocracy and royalty, and its fruit, rich in vitamin C, has long been used to make teas, marmalade and rose-hip syrup.

**Dogstooth violet**. This is in fact a member of the lily family, and was given a 'dog' name because of the shape of its tubers, which are off-white, long, shiny and pointed.

**Dog grass (also known as couch grass or twitch grass)**. Among the many grasses associated with the word 'dog', this is the one a dog aims for when feeling ill and needing to get rid of what was eaten. The dog is 'on the couch'. It has medicinal qualities for humans too – as an antiseptic and as an aid in bladder problems.

**Dog's mouth (snapdragon)**. Snapdragons have a 'mouth' which children enjoy snapping open by pressing the sides.

**Some dog superstitions:**

* If you scratch a dog before you go job-hunting, you'll get a good job.

* A strange dog walking into your house portends a new friendship.

* Meeting a dog – especially a spotted one like a Dalmatian – is considered good luck.

* A dog eating grass means it will rain soon.

* If you see three white dogs together at the same time, you will have good luck.

* If a newborn baby is licked by a dog, the baby will be a quick healer.

* If a dog scratches herself sleepily, there'll soon be a change in the weather.

* A dog which growls for no apparent reason is growling at a spirit.

Believe them if you like!

**Dogwood**. The shrubs, trees and bushes known as 'dogwoods' have stems of very hard wood, used in ancient times for making skewers and daggers. Hence it is possible that the name changed from 'dagwood' to 'dogwood' (as documented from 1548) and their berries became known as 'dogberries'.

## Dogs might wonder ...

... why humans leave the dog-toy called a 'waste-basket' with everything inside it, when it clearly needs tipping over and the contents distributing.

... why, when dogs find something deliciously fragrant to roll in, humans cry out and impose that special form of dog torture – the Bath.

... why humans act with horror when after the Bath, a dog does what his mother told him to do: shake thoroughly to get dry.

... why humans don't bury their bones and instead put them in the rubbish bin. They're clearly not safe there and can too easily be stolen by other humans.

... why people exchange pointless little 'business cards' when all they have to do is pee on a post.

... why, if a dog is a 'man's best friend', did the doctor do what he did?

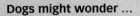

'He is my other eyes that can see above the clouds; my other ears that hear above the winds. He is the part of me that can reach out into the sea.

He has told me a thousand times over that I am his reason for being; by the way he rests against my leg; by the way he thumps his tail at my smallest smile; by the way he shows his hurt when I leave without taking him. (I think it makes him sick with worry when he is not along to care for me.)

When I am wrong, he is delighted to forgive. When I am angry, he clowns to make me smile. When I am happy, he is joy unbounded. When I am a fool, he ignores it. When I succeed, he brags.

Without him, I am only another man. With him, I am all-powerful. He is loyalty itself. He has taught me the meaning of devotion. With him, I know a secret comfort and a private peace. He has brought me understanding where before I was ignorant.

His head on my knee can heal my human hurts. His presence by my side is protection against my fears of dark and unknown things. He has promised to wait for me ... whenever ... wherever – in case I need him. And I expect I will – as I always have. He is just my dog.'

From *Tears and Laughter: A couple of dozen dog stories*, by Gene Hill

# Index

# Index of phrases

*Also by Max Cryer*

# CURIOUS ENGLISH WORDS AND PHRASES

Have you ever wondered where terms like 'Angostura bitters' and the 'green room' come from? Or why we call some people 'lounge lizards' and others 'sugar daddies'? These are just a few of the words and phrases examined by Max Cryer in this entertaining and fact-filled book. He explains where such colourful expressions come from, what they mean and how they are used. Along the way he tells a host of colourful anecdotes and dispels many myths as well. Did Sherlock Holmes really say 'Elementary my dear Watson'? And if 'ivory tower' can be found in the Bible, why has its meaning changed so drastically?

*Curious English Words and Phrases* is a treasure trove for lovers of language. Informative, amusing and excellent value for money, this book is 'the real McCoy'. From 'couch potato' to 'Bob's your uncle', you'll find the explanation here.

www.exislepublishing.com

*Also by Max Cryer*

# PREPOSTEROUS PROVERBS

We've all grown up with proverbs and we probably repeat them without much thought. Yes, 'a bird in the hand is worth two in the bush' and 'absence makes the heart grow fonder', but such sayings have almost become clichés – and it is the same in every country and culture.

In *Preposterous Proverbs*, Max Cryer looks at a vast array of proverbs from around the world on subjects ranging from birth, food, women and love to money, animals, sin and death. He has chosen some of the most interesting and perplexing, and analyses their meaning and truth with his characteristic wry wit. A great book to dip into, *Preposterous Proverbs* will take you from Greece ('A thousand men cannot undress a naked man') and Japan ('Fools and scissors must be carefully handled') to Russia ('The more you sleep, the less you sin') and India ('A fat spouse is a quilt for the winter').

www.exislepublishing.com

*Also by Max Cryer*

# WHO SAID THAT *FIRST*?

*Believe it or not*, this may well be the only book to attempt to identify the original sources of common expressions. We might think we know who first said *famous for fifteen minutes, annus horribilis, the cold war* and *let them eat cake*. A *no brainer*, you might say, but Max Cryer has a surprise or two in store for you. *I kid you not*. In this very readable book, he explores the origins of hundreds of expressions we use and hear every day – and comes up with some surprising findings. Never *economical with the truth*, he might just have *the last laugh*.

Written in Max Cryer's delightfully witty style, *Who Said That First?* is a wonderful book to dip into or settle a friendly dispute. Remember, good books are *few and far between*, and *you get what you pay for*. So *go ahead, make my day*.

www.exislepublishing.com

 e-newsletter

If you love books as much as we do, why not subscribe to our weekly e-newsletter?

As a subscriber, you'll receive special offers and discounts, be the first to hear of our exciting upcoming titles, and be kept up to date with book tours and author events. You will also receive
unique opportunities exclusive to subscribers
– and much more!

To subscribe in Australia or from any other country except New Zealand, visit
www.exislepublishing.com.au/newsletter-sign-up

For New Zealand, visit
www.exislepublishing.co.nz/newsletter-subscribe